Relating
to the most important people in your life

Tony Velie
&
Leonard Fusselman

Relating
to the most important people in your life

Henry Regnery Company • Chicago

Library of Congress Cataloging in Publication Data
Velie, Tony.
 Relating to the most important people in your life.

 1. Interpersonal relations. 2. Interpersonal
communication. I. Fusselman, Leonard, joint author.
II. Title.
HM132.V44 1976   301.11   76-6291
ISBN 0-8092-8009-4

Imperial Public Library
Imperial, Texas

Copyright © 1976 by Leonard Fusselman and Tony Velie.
All rights reserved.
Published by Henry Regnery Company
180 North Michigan Avenue, Chicago, Illinois 60601
Manufactured in the United States of America
Library of Congress Catalog Card Number: 76-6291
International Standard Book Number: 0-8092-8009-4

Published simultaneously in Canada by
Beaverbooks
953 Dillingham Road
Pickering, Ontario L1W 1Z7
Canada

To
the "George" and "Henrietta" in us all,
and to Cathy and to Max,
and to the memory of Princess Emily di Bitetto

Contents

1. On Winning and on Problems   1
2. Communications Drills   11
3. Dastardly Deeds and Failures   21
4. Standards Betrayed   33
5. Eradicating Standards   43
6. Acknowledgment and Creative Upsets   57
7. A Final Thrust at Standards   75
8. Sharing Flows   79
9. A Short Chapter on Relationships Themselves   125
10. Competition, Phase One   135
11. A Look at the Goal of Surviving: Competition, Phase Two   143
12. For the Relationship That Just Won't Go   155
13. Flowing Love   171
14. Goals to Have Together   177
    Appendix: Sexual Hangups   181

1
On Winning and on Problems

How to relate? Nothing to it, just do it. So why the rest of this book? Well, if your relationships were that smooth, you'd have something better to do than worry about them.

There are relationships that work and there are relationships that don't. The easy, unimpaired ones you just enjoy, you don't always appreciate, and you frequently ignore. After all, who's interested in the serenity of life? Not when there are sore thumbs, snagged fingers, ingrown toenails, acne, and dandruff to catch our interest and attention. Not when one worry receives more attention than 100 relaxations; not when one danger is worth a multitude of worries; not when a genuine disaster is the most priceless phenomenon of all.

(All too seldom does a worry mature into a genuinely available danger capable of bearing the spiritually interesting fruit of disaster.)

And so it goes with relationships. When two humans can have each other exactly the way he or she is, then they have a happy thing going—providing each has sense enough to appreciate the other and to leave well enough alone. But this kind of life-enhancing intelligence is rare, and so are gratifying relationships. If you can enjoy a live-and-let-live relationship with your mate, your business partner, your parents, or your kids, don't bother with the drills in this book; they are not directed at you.

Relating and Winning

The drills in this book operate on the premise that even an average-size giant is taller than a huge pygmy. *So its drills are out to turn pygmies into giants.* What this means is that a tradition gets overthrown in our book: If you are willing to engage your time and your attention in our drills, you will get to a space where *your entire concept of winning and losing undergoes a dramatic change.*

Traditionally, "I"—in order to win—have had to do "my" winning at "your" expense. "I" have had, in other words, to exploit "you." And as "you" have sunk, "I" (and my faithful dog named Ego) have appeared to rise. And traditionally, too, most of the so-called winners have achieved their lofty state of winning by reducing others to pygmy-size and then by treading on their necks and stomping on the bowed backs. (One of the earliest pieces of art still in existence in the Western world shows Naram-Sin, the Mesopotamian king, standing on the necks of kings of neighboring peoples whom his armies had conquered.) For at least the last 5,000 years, the way to win was deprive "you" of as much being as "I" could get away with. Me, Naram-Sin, you slave; me Tarzan, you Jane—clean out the treehouse.

But there is another equally pragmatic and infinitely more pleasurable way to win: "I" can pump "you" up (and all of the other "you's" around me) so that we all start feeling so good and being so high that we all rise together. The drills in this book provide sufficient spiritual helium for "you" to win and to rise along with "me."

The traditional method of "my" winning at "your" expense just doesn't work very well any more. We all know too much about each others' intentions, about our capacity to enslave, and about the technological means of instituting a global slavery. "My" oppressing and repressing "you" simply isn't effective any longer. "You" can always revolt and turn the tables on me. Short of totally annihilating "you," then, the more practical course would be for both of us to create a state of *mutual winning*.

This idea is so fundamentally simple that, complex creature that you are, gentle reader, perhaps it bears repeating. . . . If "I" spend my time putting "you" down, our relationship degenerates into one of "I" win/"you" lose (ha-ha-ha). And if this form of relationship continues for a long enough time, *both of us* will become frozen in these roles. Now, since the very ties that bind us depend on "your" abasement, sooner or later "I" am going to quit rising at "your" expense. And shortly after this happens, "I" am going to start to sink myself. Examine the lurid pages of history and see if this has not been the fundamental flaw of all life-denying civilizations, i.e., those that have been based on brute force.

A psychic umbilical cord (which, later in the text, we will refer to as a "flow") seems to bind relationships. Do not let the very simplicity of this concept confuse you. "You" and "I" are joined in a relationship. If "I" am continually oppressing and repressing "you," then, in a relatively short period of time, "I" will be right down there in the muck alongside "you." It's the old paradox of the slave master becoming enslaved by slavery.

However, this "psychic umbilical cord" is infinitely pliable, and if "I," in our relationship, act in a manner that enhances "your" being, "I" cannot help but have my being enhanced, too, because "you" will appreciate and enjoy "me." *Do unto others as you would have them do unto you.* . . . This is all that my coauthor and I mean when we talk about Winning Relationships: "I" do not have to have "my" ego inflated at "your" expense. I put gas in your car; you put gas in mine. Together, we can either co-destruct or co-create. The choice is ours.

Winning Co-creations Beget Increasing Wins

Hitler, for example, did a lot for an apathetic Germany. As long as he was pumping up the Fatherland and validating his own particular group's greatness, he enjoyed a meteoric rise and so did his party. But when he began putting more people down than he was pumping up, a global put-down contest developed and Hitler sank to the level of a concrete bunker.

Losing Co-creations Create Increasing Losses

A global put-down contest on the scale of WW II created an enormous amount of loss for everyone concerned. If today's inflation bothers you, take a look at when and why we began stockpiling our staggeringly huge national debt. Or take a quick look at Richard Nixon: He did not pump up his own people. Thus, shortly after they started going down the tube he followed suit. Or look at U.S. involvement with corrupt regimes in Indochina during the past couple of decades. Our country made the mistake of backing men who only took from their people and who gave them nothing in return. This governmental policy was not supported by a sufficient number of U.S. citizens, and it very nearly brought this country to a state of civil war. (Indeed, it's possible that when the history of the latter part of this century is written the Vietnam debacle may be seen as the beginning of the decline of U.S. power and influence.)

All that we wish to convey to you is this: When "my" trip is that of creating *enhanced being* for "my" particular partner or group, "I" will inevitably rise—because creating the positive puts us all in a positive space. I flow positive, life-enhancing creations to you; you flow them back to me; and the limits as to how far both of us can rise appear to be infinite only because they are unknown. (Unfortunately, nobody has really ever started playing this kind of we-both-win-together game long enough to ascertain its peak. But this does not have to mean that we can't start, does it?)

So why lose in your relationships any longer? True, losses are the area where the action is, but if the 1930s and 1940s and 1950s and 1960s and half of the 1970s haven't given you sufficient action, then you are truly a glutton for punishment, and you don't need the drills in this book; you need, instead, a year's membership in a bondage and dominance parlor or the unique opportunity to do some motocross with your local chapter of the Hell's Angels.

So, loss-lovers, be warned: *The techniques in this book put you in a space of conscious choice, cause over, and control of those relationships you wish to have.* A lot of your games will go—out the top—and all you'll have for disasters are an occasional toothache or grouch that you let get past your vigilance. Hang on them! They're all that's between you and daytime TV.

Primarily, the thrust of this book is on the male-female thing because the battle of the sexes interests my coauthor and me the most. But the techniques and technology in this book are by no means confined to Blondie-Dagwood (or Edith vs. Archie) disputes. They apply equally as well to what goes on (or does not go on) between children and their parents; brothers and their sisters; employers and employees; old, greatly admired hero or heroine-types and your seeming inconsequence compared to these paragons; as well as old, traditional antagonists to whom you are seemingly locked "forever" in the I'm-Right-Your're-Wrong relationship one psychologist or another has labeled "love-hate." The drills in this book will bring you, if such is your case, to a psychospiritual space where you don't necessarily love thine enemy, but where *you cease creating the other as an automatic enemy to begin with.* And when you see that other exactly as he or she is, the options to love him/her or to leave him/her strictly alone, or to love him/her close up or at a distance will be yours.

Target Fixations

Now, we said earlier that losses are where the action accumulates. The reason for this is because problems intrigue our species.

Those problems which we feel we have to have but want no part of might be referred to as *negativities*. Ninety-nine percent of the time, these negativities are compulsive attention-getters:

> "My, what a lovely rose. I'll sniff it—Omigod! A spider! Chills run up and down my spine. Where'd the thing go? In the cuff of my pants? Is it crawling on me right now? I really love flowers, and someday I'll get interested in horticulture, if only I can get over my spider-phobia."

In this example, our hypothetical nature-lover voluntarily chooses to be interested in flowers but does not choose to direct his attention anywhere near spiders. Yet which of the two receives the vast preponderance of his interest and attention?

> "Sure, we've got enough money in the bank to pay the rent next week and buy groceries, but suppose the car breaks down? Then we'd really be in bad shape. So let's not drive to Disneyland as planned because if that car breaks down on the freeway, we've had it...."

Guess what's going to occupy this citizen's attention all weekend long.

Most of us are very conservative, and we exhaust ourselves trying to stay protected from problems that *might happen* instead of creating enjoyments to participate in. The entire phenomenon is known as *target fixation.*

> Here I am tooling down the highway on my Kawasaki Zero Avenger at 90 mph, surrounded by 360° of emptiness, and I have no problems. But put a turtle on the road ahead, and a problem of survival is immediately created for me-the-motorcyclist, and I will put my attention on that turtle. Depending on the kind of shape I'm in spiritually and psychologically, I will either narrowly miss it or run right into it and wrack the turtle, the bike, and my body up.

Watch two couples on a dance floor or two skiers on a slope—it is as if they are bound to one another by an overwhelmingly powerful magnetism. Given a large amount of room to operate in, they will invariably come very close or actually collide. Problems exert the same kind of stranglehold over us all.

Let us expand our generalization and say that, usually, *all problems that appear to exercise a compulsive hold over our attention are survival-oriented,* because the instant we consider survival itself a problem, survival becomes one. (Read the last part of this sentence carefully and file it away for future reference. It is not gibberish.)

> Our argument is proceeding as follows:
> Whatever we consider to be a problem becomes a problem; and problems fascinate us; and negativities (which are problems we

feel we have to have but want no part of) persist automatically while joys do not.

Joys we do not mind having, and so they come and they go of their own accord. Negativities we do mind having and we begrudge any attention we pay them, and so they persist.

Whence we draw this following psychic law:

WHATEVER YOU, OR I, OR THE GUY DOWN THE BLOCK RESISTS HAVING EXACTLY AS IT IS, WILL PERSIST.

What this law has to do with relationships is this: *The so-called negativity of another person is inordinately demanding of my attention because of the target-fixation syndrome.* For example:

> "My" Henrietta has a beautiful body and a face off the cover of a movie magazine and is passionate and has a giving nature. From my point of view, she has four (count 'em) positive qualities. Her so-called one negative quality (from my point of view) is that she bestows all this beauty and passion on Larry and Barry and Harry and Jerry. Result? I don't see Henrietta anymore.

Her one negative attribute cancels out her beautiful face, her panting Pavlovian bell of a figure, her passion, and her generosity. I cannot stand sharing her favors, and even though I love Henrietta, I avoid seeing her face-to-face and spend all my time thinking about her. This is not bright. This is dumb, in fact, and this is pretty much the way of the world.

If someone you know has nine "positive" qualities and *one* "negative" quality, you will feel lukewarm toward him or her. ("Oh yeah, old George is okay. I don't see much of him. . . .") *Because we-the-species tend to fixate on what we consider to be negative qualities in others because anything negative can mean a threat to survival.*

Negativity is an automatic attention-getter. For instance, there has never been a horror movie that lost its producer's money. Never. Or, speaking of movies, consider the glorious Raquel Welch.

Drill

Right now, in your mind's eye, picture Raquel very clearly. Here she is; by consensus vote of most males, the most glamorous star in Hollywood. Okay, now . . . put a wart on the tip of her nose. Do this mentally: Put a wart on the fantastic Raquel's gorgeous nose. See it there. Now, see all of Ms. Welch's face and figure. What do you fixate on? Her smooth limbs? Her undulant belly? Her silky hair? Her sensual mouth? Her white teeth? Un unh. You look at the wart. *Cease creating these pictures.*

My coauthor and I have taken the liberty of defacing a national monument only to underline our thesis that, as a species, our considerations of what is negative will *always* outweigh those qualities in another which we consider positive. (Although, in fairness, with someone as utterly gorgeous as Raquel, it would probably take up to half-a-dozen warts strategically placed over her face and body to give most males pause.) *Negativity is more interesting to the vast majority of us.* Which is more interesting to you? A rose or a tarantula? (Can a rose bite you?)

"The evil men do" (which is usually more interesting than their philanthropies) "lives after them. The good is oft interred with their bones . . ." observed Marc Antony, and he was absolutely right.

Negativity automates itself because we are profoundly interested in the game of survival on this planet, and just about everything we consider negative constitutes a threat to future survival. For this reason, it is hard for *any* of us to have and to maintain a winning relationship with someone else or a whole group of someone elses. We get restless. We get bored, and we get out.

This theme will be pursued later on at some length.

Problems

Let us define problems as "something you want, but don't have; or as something you have, but don't want."

This definition cuts across the general boundary lines of all types of relationships and further breaks down into a whole gamut of upsets, from the "We Have a Raging Fight Everytime I Mention My Ex-boyfriend," through "I Can't Stand *them* and *they* Can't Stand Me," through "I Like You and I Respect Your Intelligence, So Why Are We Always Working at Cross-Purposes," right on down to "We Sure Bore Each Other" and "Everything We Put Our Hands on Turns to Shit.". . . This gamut of problems will be found in any sort of relationship—sexual, financial, etc.—that is not being engaged in cheerfully by at least one of the relators.

The drills in this book are out to handle any of these relationships, and they do this by encouraging you to look at the problems so thoroughly that they lose their problematic quality and become games you are free to play or not to play. The choice is yours. Of course, it always has been, but you probably have not been ready to assume the responsibility for making this choice because

BELIEVE IT OR NOT

—you are what you are, because that is what you are being, doing, and having. If you are upset with Henrietta for spending a lot of time in other men's beds, who's creating that upset? *You* are.

If you're upset with my coauthor and me for being so pratingly obvious (and also for having you picture Raquel with a wart on her nose—is nothing sacred?), *you* are creating your upset.

Your upsets are *yours;* mine are *mine* (who else could possibly create them?)

So the thrust of all the drills in this liberating volume will be in the direction of your seeing—which is far, far senior to believing—that *you are at cause over your own fouled-up relationships,* and of your also seeing that you can get to a space where *you can have (or not have) and maintain (or not maintain) any relationship with anybody you care to.* You can, in other words, arrive at a spiritual and psychological space (which you will have created) where you will be free enough to take relationships or leave them alone. *There will be a choice, and the choice will be yours.*

2
Communications Drills

Whatever you are in relationship with you are, to some degree (great or small), at cause over. If a tiger is chasing you, you are within visual, olfactory, and pre-gustatory cause over its developing an appetite—and if you happen to be that tiger, then you are at a great degree of cause over yonder yummy morsel currently comparing his four-minute mile to your three-minute mile. However, if you and the tiger did not happen to notice each other, then there is no exchange of communication between the two of you, hence there can be no exchange of creativity between the two of you. The tiger missed a meal, and your day is that much duller.

Any Exchange of Creativity Is Communication
... a kiss, a punch in the nose, a letter, actions, deeds are all communications.

Assumptions, expectations, secrets are not communications. *Whatever is withheld and not communicated usually tends to destroy relationships.* For example:

a) George dislikes the scent of Henrietta's perfume but

b) is too much of a "gentleman" to tell her this (or he doesn't want to hurt her feelings and so withholds this bit of information)
so
c) George puts a lot of distance between self and Henrietta, causing
d) Henrietta to wonder if she smells bad and begins
e) dousing herself in perfume by the bucketful, which brings about
f) George not seeing very much of Henrietta any more.

A relationship is endangered, when a mere, "Henrietta, you smell so sweet anyway' you don't need to wear perfume" probably could have avoided the upset between the two lovers.

Add to this the fact that George mows the lawn almost every morning before going off to work because he assumes Henrietta is so proud of her home, and the fact that the sound of a power mower underneath her window nearly drives Henrietta up the wall, but she doesn't say anything about this because she *assumes* George is so proud of his home (while actually neither of them could care less about the shape their lawn is in), and you have another stepping stone in the lonely road to Heartbreak Hotel.

Now, granted the above two examples of George's and Henrietta's problems are in themselves light (and easily handled), but imagine that there exist fifty-eight similar minor upsets between the two—fifty-eight single, separate items on which the truth is withheld; enough little soldiers to start a war—and the relationship is imperiled.

The following drill is out to eradicate all the "inconsequential little items" that grow up (molehills to mountains) between two formerly close people.

Ask someone with whom you are no longer communicating too well the following question over and over again until the mountain has become a molehill again, or perhaps even a divot:

— DRILL NO. ONE —

a) "What don't you like about me?"

Continue asking your partner this question until he or she

has pulled up and viewed and re-viewed all of your minor foibles and flaws. Note that it is important for you to acknowledge each of the answers your partner gives each time you ask this leading question. Note, too, that acknowledgment does not imply agreement; it merely signifies that you have received your partner's communication.

After he or she has told you everything he or she doesn't like about you, the time comes for you to switch roles. It is now your partner's turn to put this same question—"What don't you like about me?"—to you over and over and over again, acknowledging each and every answer you make, until you are communicating freely with him or her.

Changing one's ways is by no means the prime benefit derived from this drill. The truly big victory this drill gives you both is that, when this drill is run long enough, you both begin communicating with and understanding each other. This is most noticeable as a change of attitude or atmosphere between and surrounding the two of you. Subliminally, George's feelings toward the beleaguered Henrietta will change and Henrietta's subliminal feelings toward the maligned George will change. Whether they live happily together forever and ever becomes slightly more *in the range of their conscious choice*.

Variation on Drill One (to be used when appropriate) is as follows:

b) What don't you like about our _____?
(Fill in the blank with what feels most appropriate to you and your partner. For instance:
   marriage
   relationship
   affair
   partnership
   deal (big or small)
... or whatever you and your partner feel should go in that blank).

Drill One and its variation are always run two ways: *i.e.,* from you to the other person and from the other person to you.
FOR EXAMPLE
   George and Henrietta sit down.

GEORGE: Henrietta, what don't you like about me?
HENRIETTA: You're always eating graham crackers in bed.
GEORGE: Okay. I heard that. (This is an acknowledgment; it does not imply that George agrees with Henrietta, merely that he's heard her. He then asks the same question again.)
GEORGE: Henrietta, what don't you like about me? (She answers; he acknowledges hearing her answer, then asks the question again.)

And he continues asking this question until she has exhausted all the negative traits of George's which she dislikes. Once she's got them all (and this drill takes as long to run as it takes to run, and not one moment more), they switch places. It is now Henrietta's turn to ask her partner: "George, what don't you like about me?" and to acknowledge his answer, and to continue asking this question until he has enumerated everything he dislikes about her. "Thank you"; "Okay"; "Got that"; and "I heard that" are all acknowledgments.

Instructive Factors for Running the Variation on Drill One

This is not a place to defend. This is not a place to accuse or make yourself or anyone else right or wrong—above all this drill (and its predecessor) should not be used as arenas in which to stage arguments.

The *only* appropriate communications to this drill ("What don't you like about our _____ ?") are:
 a) the question
 b) the answer
 c) and the acknowledgment. "Okay." "All right." "Thank you" or "I got that" are all appropriate acknowledgments. They mean only "I heard and understood what you just said."
Other communications are merely dramatizations related to the dislikes in question.
Dramatizations are communications—yes. But, in these two drills dramatizations are inappropriate.

In Other Words

Dramatizations are the crap that probably brought about George's and Henrietta's upsets with each other to begin with.

So park them and do Drill One and, if appropriate, its variation. If you want to dramatize and sell someone else your point of view, get a job on a used-car lot. If you wouldn't mind initiating a relationship that flows smoothly between you and your partner, run this drill verbatim.

For That So and So You Can't Talk To

If there is someone you absolutely cannot bring yourself to express yourself to, the following drill resolves this difficulty.

A person is only a person, and that's no problem. Without getting into whys and their attendant complications for the time being, let us merely say that there are often individuals with whom there is little or no communication. The inhibitors to direct communication are many and varied. Frequently these inhibitions assume the form of emotional or intuitive themes involving fear, anger, distrust, etc. The only consistency towards these people with whom we cannot communicate is the great wealth of non- or mis-communications to and/or from this person. These areas of impossible communicators fall into various categories—for instance, some of us find it well nigh impossible to talk to our parents; others of us cannot talk to such Authority Figures as cops or teachers. And some of us also have entire subject areas (like sex or money or our real feelings) which we absolutely cannot bring ourselves to discuss with anyone, not even those closest to us.

— DRILL NO. TWO: Mental Images —

If you find that you have an inhibited flow of communication with a person or institution then,

Step One: Make a very solid mental image of that person or that particular institution (the I.R.S., for instance, or the assembly line on which you are but a social security number) and bring him, her, or it into the same room with you, close enough to talk to.

Step Two: Ask yourself the following question, verbatim: "If you could freely express yourself to _____, what would you say or do?"

Step Three: Once you have decided what you would say or do to that hated, feared, mistrusted, or disliked other, comes the time to make this communication to him, her, or it.

Do this right now. Express yourself to that person or that institution.

Step Four: Continue to express yourself until you are freely communicating with the formerly hated or feared other.

This particular drill has put more people back on speaking terms than singing telegrams. Some of you will have no trouble at all putting out a mental picture of another whom you would rather not talk to. Others of you will find this extremely difficult to do. If you fall into this latter category and truly cannot see yourself sharing any space whatever with, let us say, your father, yet you know that there are a great many unfinished communications between the two of you, then you might try a little ploy. Remember: This is merely a matter of imagination. . . .

Picture the person whom you need to communicate with, but for any number of good reasons you can't bring yourself to talk to, standing in the doorway to your home. Mentally create a tennis ball and toss it to him or her. Have him or her catch it and toss it back to you. Continue tossing the imaginary tennis ball back and forth until the "two" of you are in the same room. Note that my coauthor and I understand your reservations about this little mind game. At first glance, it does seem a rather strange thing to do, but we ask you to do it for at least three reasons. These being:

1. That any person whom you will not communicate with has you. Your relationship with that other is both stagnant and frozen. It cannot change. You will continue to hate him or fear him (or her) for as long as you live.
2. You cannot take charge of a relationship and get to feel free of it as long as it remains frozen.
3. If you make no effort to assume responsibility over your share of the ridge of blocked communications between you and that other, you will be holding that ridge in place. The ridge may consist of resentment, fear, anger, hate, contempt, hurt pride—a whole catalog of woes—and if you make no effort to change your creativity regarding it, it will persist. And you will never be able to feel good about that particular other. Never.

Communications Drills

Opening channels of communication between you and a so-called enemy is the first step you can take toward freeing yourself. It is a giant one.

In this imaginative drill, the inability to create a mental picture of another and to confront him or her does not happen all that often. But it does come up frequently enough for us to go on at some length about the importance of your being willing to do it. Many and varied are the manifestations of this communicative impossibility, but always consistent is the fact that *I just can't talk to that s.o.b.! It just won't work!* Great waves of overwhelming I-give-up will put you out of business from the start. If these waves come up, acknowledge their presence and realize that they will in no way diminish the effectiveness of the drill if handled in the following manner:

a) Create a mental image picture of that antagonist;
b) Create a mental picture of a tennis ball and start playing a game of catch with your antagonist. Do this for several minutes.
c) Then try talking to him or her again. By now, your communication should flow a lot more easily.
d) If even this doesn't serve to bring you into communication with an imaginary, other, then begin mentally creating larger spheres—say, basketballs—to toss back and forth. Do this for several minutes, then change the basketballs into anvils and mentally toss them back and forth between the two of you. After another couple of minutes, transform the basketballs into something huge and improbable like dump trucks and begin tossing them back and forth at the rate of several per second. All that this requires is a little imagination, and imagination is a commodity of which you possess an unlimited supply.

The net effect of doing this imaginary tossing of increasingly large objects to and fro is to overwhelm the blockage of the smooth flow of communication between you and your antagonist. This blockage formerly overwhelmed you because it consisted of so many single, separate incidents of mistrust, anger, hurt, etc. But now your willingness to confront your antagonist mentally and to communicate with him or her has won out. Is this clear?

As we indicated before, such radical handling of a blocked communications flow will not need to be used for very many people, but it's nice to know that it exists.

The newfound freedom to communicate which will be achieved through this drill invariably puts another person into your world. For example: A client of my coauthor's was a 22-year-old young man whose chief drawback to talking to his father was indecision: He didn't know whether to hit the old man or to run off screaming. Hence there was little communication between father and son. Clearing father as a person to relate to put the young man back in the family to a point where he cut his hair, gave up his guitar and part-time welding job, and followed his father's advice by attending school for budding investment brokers. He lasted there about three months before returning to what he wanted to do which was play the guitar and arc weld, but at least now he, his guitar, and his father all have a nice relationship.

Types of Communications Terminals

For types of communications terminals to whom you have problems relating (I am a terminal; my coauthor is a terminal; you are a terminal; your boss is a terminal, etc.), survey your life experience for inhibitions. For example, physical types—some people are choked up over pretty girls (they see one and stammer, stutter, hem, haw, fidget, and foul up). Other people feel they cannot talk to ugly girls, old people, anyone black, anyone white, and so forth and so on . . . judges, dentists. So search your experience now for *types* of people with whom you feel a limited ability to communicate. Once you spot a particular problem area, mentally create an ideal representative of this particular type. Then perform the same drill on him or her or it—communicate freely everything you've always wanted to say or do.

One of the strangest cases my coauthor ever worked on was that of a police officer whose particular ridge of blocked communications flow was with uniformed policemen in general and "tough cops" in particular. Needless to say, the difference his running this drill made in his professional relationships was noticeable to himself, his fellow peace officers, and the M.D. who was treating his ulcer.

The vast majority of my coauthor's experiences with this drill are less bizarre but by no means less outstanding as far as results achieved.

Subject Area

"I hate to talk shop!"

"Can't stand all this gossip!"

"All men ever want to talk about is sex. It just drives me crazy!"

"Edith, will you and Maude take your girl talk someplace else?"

There are as many varieties of inhibited subjects of communication as there are types of people. If you hate to talk about golf, then your relationship with golfers is going to be inhibited. A limited ability to express yourself on the subject of _____ (astrology/binary computers/bowling/fashion/food/politics, etc.) cuts you off from the possibility of getting to know that many more people and perhaps discovering that you truly like one or two of them.

If you are afflicted with an extremely loathsome subject area about which you have enormously strong antipathies, the quickest way to bring yourself into a space where you can see the subject for what it is and then decide whether it's worth the bother to acquire any interest in is to:

a) Create a mental image picture of a friend of yours and then talk to him or her at some length about this particular subject.
b) Continue talking about this subject until the taboo (if there is one) is off it or until you are communicating about it in a free, flowing manner.

The acid test for these drills is actually talking to that specific person or to the specific types of persons or about a certain subject matter you loathed—and seeing how well you do. So after running these drills, look up the object of your mental imagery in person and test your newfound ability to communicate. If the results are totally free, enjoy your victory; if your relationship with the other is changed but is still inhibited, go back and run the appropriate drill some more. If your relationship with the other has changed very little, run the appropriate drill *many* more times. The only indication to bypass this particular communication terminal is when the drill does produce a distinct change in your relation to him or to her (or it), yet the limitation to freely communicating with him or her still persists in a much altered form. If this is so, you have definitely expanded the gain-producing potential of this drill and the remaining inhibitions persisting are from a totally different area of relational aberrations and are to be handled by other, appropriate drills which we will present later on in the test.

For example: "I've never been able to talk to my boss and I've always hated him, but I needed the job and couldn't quit. Consciously or otherwise, I ripped the company off for over a dozen paper clips a week for the last twenty-seven years. This amounts to nearly $18.70. I can talk freely to the boss now, but I feel like such a crook that I'm ashamed of myself. How can I get that handled, short of confessing or paying back the $18.70?"

Read the rest of this book, do its drills, and you'll have the opportunity of becoming a kingpin in the hot office-supplies racket.

3

Dastardly Deeds and Failures

There's more to relating than shooting the breeze: "Baby, I didn't come here just to talk". Hitler, for instance, was a great communicator, but not too many people got along with him. It could be said that there was something wrong with his relationships toward the rest of the world. He had a lot to say, and a lot to say it with—loudspeakers, panzer divisions, the Luftwaffe—but his fan club will never approximate the Rolling Stones'. Some of the reasons why communications "go wrong" is the subject of this chapter.

In a previous book, *Mind Games,* we went into great detail about a piece of mental machinery we all have that is not bright enough to tie its own shoelaces. We called it "The Automatic Mind." Volumes could be written about it, but what we want to say about it can be said very concisely: The following drills deal directly with this literal, dumb, and extremely powerful piece of your mind that is the blueprint of lifetimes, civilizations, planets, galaxies. Discrimination is not its forte. It is a comparer, not a differentiator. For example: "I love roses. I could really get into the pleasure of cultivating and appreciating those beautiful flowers. If it weren't for the spiders that make me shiver. (I shiver automatically.) When something crawly gets on my skin, I automatically startle (I don't think about it, I just jump). I never stop to realize that I am a million times more dangerous to these little eight-legged crawlies than they are to me, but deadly they are because they make me dangerous to myself." (Spiders have brought about more fractures and contusions than street-fighting.)

The citizen in our previous chapter who has ripped off almost nineteen dollars worth of paper clips is going to equate himself subliminally with an infinity of thievery, guilt, shame, blame, and regret despite the fact that his firm thinks so highly of him that he has but to ask and a whole paper-clip factory would be his. The housewife who secretly lusts after Robert Redford's body and who once smoked a Virginia Slim while leafing through a *Playgirl* magazine is unjustly accusing herself of being Queen Wanton. Unreasonably and more often than not, unconsciously, such a feeling is there. This feeling does overlap to some degree with the conscious creativity of a relationship. Frequently, individuals have committed or do commit actual overt acts of hostility against another. When these actions go undetected, *i.e.*, no one knows about them but yourself, you have that action—plus all those unconscious, nonrational comparisons—as a barrier between you and your relationship partner.

The same machinery that makes you shiver when you pick a rose with a spider in it is the one that summons forth the shadow army when you commit an iniquity against another person—whether this iniquity be detected or not. This shadow army of somewhat similar deeds or occurrences stands between your freely sharing your creativity with another. ("What was that that just crossed your mind, dear?" "Shut up, you dumb sonofabitch, and mind your own business.") This shadow army depletes from your wholeness and makes sure that, when it is marching across your spectrum of consciousness, there will be considerably less of you available to share with another. There have been many labels and brand names attached to this shadow army: Guilt; Karma; the Ego-antagonistic Id; the Devil. . . . My coauthor and I are calling it "The Automatic Mind." It is only what it is. *But* what it *represents,* either consciously or otherwise, virtually ensures the impairment of your ability to see clearly what is happening around you and to act appropriately. It is a mouse in monster's clothing ("it's the principle of the thing"), but it is also one of the building blocks of the automatic persistence of the physical universe.

The following drills and their variations put you in an intuitive "I'm Not Such A Bad Guy After All" place in relation to those whom you run the drills about. They will remove the psychic spiders from the overlap of your life and that of whomever you run the drills in relation to.

Instructions for Running These Drills

There are, depending upon your current life's circumstances, three ways to go in running these drills: 1) alone; 2) with a partner who will take the time to ask you the questions and to acknowledge your answers, and to continue asking you the same set of questions over and over until you divest yourself of all the overt or covert dastardly deeds you may be accusing yourself of; 3) with *the* partner . . . that person with whom you are sharing a life and experiencing difficulties, or a business relationship and its attendant "It's All *Your* Faults."

Working Alone

If you, poor you, are isolated and have no one who will bother to run this drill with you (or if you are alone because what you've done is so terrible that you can't bring yourself to admit it to another), or if you are merely alone out of perference, and you've got a relational problem with somebody else, ask yourself the following four questions in this order, repetitively, until you really feel good about the other person. This is to say, you're in the kind of brawny emotional shape where you can pick up the phone and say—and really mean—"Hey, so & so! It's me! I miss you! Haven't seen you for too long. Let's have dinner Tuesday night." *As opposed to* "O God, I want to call so and so, but after all that's happened between us, I know so and so'll never speak to me again."

question a)   "What's not all right about my relationship with _____?"

In the blank space provided, you will put his or her name.

1. answer the question.
2. acknowledge your answer.* "Thank you"; "I got that"; "I heard that" are all acknowledgments; they do (let us repeat) *not* indicate agreement, but are merely the formal indication that the communication was received.
3. move on to the next question.

question b) "In relation to _____, what failures have occurred?"
1. answer this question.
2. acknowledge your answer.
3. move on to the next question.

question c) "What have I done to _____ that's not all right?"
1. answer this question.
2. acknowledge your answer.
3. move on to the next question.

question d) "How have I failed _____?"
1. answer the question.
2. acknowledge your answer.
3. move on to question a) which you ask yourself again as if for the first time.

Listen Carefully Now

The reason my coauthor and I have you go over and over the questions is because the problems you are experiencing right here/right now have their roots buried deep in the past. Extremely deep. It is by taking the time to ask yourself the questions over and over that you eventually arrive at the roots of your hangups. Once you eradicate these, you become proportionately more free. Consider the very repetition of these questions as a form of guided meditation; the questions remain the same. Each time one of them is asked again, the answer will be slightly different. And it is the bulk of all your answers to these questions that impedes and impairs your relationship with the name

---

*To state the obvious: Every communication cycle has, like Greek tragedy, a beginning; a middle, and an end. The acknowledgment is important because it brings to an end one communication cycle. It is important to complete each and every cycle you undertake because, unless you are in supremely good psychological and spiritual shape, the incomplete cycle will "hang up" a certain amount of your attention indefinitely. All this is gone into laboriously in our previous book, *Mind Games*.

you are placing in the blank spaces. Reality is formless and in flux and confusing. The questions, being constant, are form-ful; *i.e.*, they have the effect of putting a kind of net over the elusive stuff of experience. Their very constancy gives you the chance to pull yourself, hand-by-hand so to speak, over the confusing flux of experience and to arrive at a point where you can have certainty about where you stand in regard to another.

So these questions are tools, really, to help you file your experiences with someone else in their proper order in space and in time. They give you handholds over a great abyss. Eventually, if they are asked in this order, answered honestly, and acknowledged properly, these questions will take you to a space where you can clearly see what your relationship with that other is and where, in today's vernacular, it's at. Amen.

Working with a Partner

If you are fortunate enough to have a friend who will agree to spare you forty-five minutes to an hour-and-a-half of his or her time, then have him or her run you through this drill as follows:

Your partner sits down opposite you; let us assume that there is a table between the two of you, though there need not be. Making good eye contact with you, your partner says, "We are about to begin the session—is there something I should know about you but don't?

Answer your partner truthfully.

Your partner then asks you: "Is there any reason why we can't run this session for the next forty-five minutes or so uninterruptedly?"

Again, answer him truthfully. This might be a good time to take your phone off its cradle.

Once the air is cleared between you, your partner asks you one last question, which is:

question a):   "Tell me the name of the person with whom your relationship is not smoothly flowing."
1. Answer him.*

---

*Here comes a sexist cop-out. I don't like writing instructions, neither does my co-author. They are tedious for us; we already know how to run these drills. Rather than say each time *have him or her* acknowledge you, it is easier for us to write *have your partner* or *have him* say thus and so. This is why we will often refer to the person helping you with our drills in the masculine gender. Sheer laziness.

2. Have your partner acknowledge your answer.

Placing the name you have given your partner in the blank space provided, your partner then asks you:

question b): "What's not all right about your relationship with _____?"
1. You answer.
2. He acknowledges you.
3. He then asks:

question c): "In relation to your _____ (marriage/affair/business deal, etc.—whatever term is appropriate) with _____, what failures have occurred?"
1. Answer your partner.
2. He acknowledges receipt of your answer.
3. He moves on to:

question d): "What have you done to _____ that's not all right?"
1. Answer your partner; tell him what you've done to your wife or girl friend or business associate that's not all right.
2. He acknowledges hearing your answer.
3. He moves on to:

question e): "How have you failed _____?"
1. You answer.
2. He acknowledges your answer.
3. He returns to question b) again, and you both continue cycling through this drill about your iniquities toward and failures with good old _____ until you divest yourself of the burden of guilt or that mountain of apprehension that had been standing between you and _____ and obscuring _____ from your view.

In other words, you continue being cycled through this drill until you feel pretty good about _____ and can see both him/her exactly as he/she is and you also see your relationship with _____ exactly as it is.

Working with THE Partner

This is perhaps the most effective of any single technique; also it is frequently the most difficult. Presumably communication is impeded between you and your special other (your man; your lady) and the impasses between the two of you which have been dealt with in the two previous chapters are no longer standing between you and him or her. The earlier drills, in other words, have brought you to a point where you can sit down and talk to your special terminal. We hope so because this drill offers the greatest temptation to argue, defend, dramatize how right you are (and how wrong your special terminal is), and, in general, not confront the creations standing between the two of you. It is at this point imperative that you and your partner—both entirely of your own volition, with no help or prompting from the other—be totally aware of, acknowledge, and understand each and every communication that passes between you. This does not mean that you agree with what the other says. This does not imply that you sympathize with or condone the other's point of view, but merely that both of you understand and be aware of what the other is saying. To argue or to try to sell your point of view in this drill defeats it entirely and blows it right down the same tube your relationship has been going down.

The necessity to defend and dramatize is what corrodes even the most gold-plated relationship. So resist this temptation and just stick to the drill.

a) On a 3" by 5" index card or sheet of paper, write the following questions:
   1. "What have I done to you that's not all right?"
   2. "How have I failed you?"
   3. "What have you done to me that's not all right?"
   4. "How have you failed me?"

These four questions are all that goes on the card. These are the *only* questions that are asked. The only questions answered are those that are asked, and each question is answered.

Do *not* buy a "nothing" or an "everything's all right." If everything were all right between the two of you, why have you embarked upon this drill?

When it is your turn to ask one of these questions, do not be pushy; be patient. There is an answer to every question, no matter how insignificant (or important) the answer may seem.

The only acknowledgment necessary for each answer is: "Thank you." Anything else than delivering these questions verbatim partakes of the same old run-around that got you here in the first place.

Each question is read aloud by one partner to the other, who then answers it. The partner asking the question acknowledges the answer, then moves on to the next question.

When all four questions have been read off, answered, and acknowledged, then the partner who was asking the questions hands the card to the partner who was answering them. It is now this partner's turn to ask the other the four questions and to acknowledge each and every answer made.

Continue cycling through this drill, exchanging the card at the end of each drill cycle until the relationship between the two of you is significantly changed for the better.

As stated before, this change is more often than not perceived intuitively; invariably it becomes apparent in the near future.

This drill takes as long to run as it takes. Run it until both you and your partner start looking and feeling a lot better, and there is a good deal of warmth between the two of you. And remember, running this drill "too long" is never a waste of either your time or your partner's. Running it not long enough always is.

A California couple (he was bisexual; she was straight) came to my coauthor for a little bit of counseling. They had a sexual difference of opinion and the jealousy was flashing like a bullfighter's cape in the sunshine. He claimed that he was faithful to his wife as long as he didn't bed other women—but guys, they didn't count. She thought that anyone else whom he was making love with was a rival and an enemy. Some ninety minutes through this drill, run under the auspices of my coauthor, brought them to a point where they were (and are) sharing the same bed, not always with the same people, but with each other more often than not, and their marriage continues in an unexpectedly happy vein.

Another couple was less a flagrant example of "the new morality": Her predilection for needlepoint drove him to backpacking, which drove her to burning the breakfast (nattering away with curlers in her hair) and creating a beautiful tapestry—which in turn drove him to becoming a middleweight authority on Pueblo and American Indian artifacts, which necessitated his frequent absences on field trips, these bringing about their "What-the-hell-let's-give-this-drill-a-try" as a predivorce maneuver. Today, they do a lot of sedate living and loving, with a lot of quiet good times together, while she does her needlepoint (and their child fits neatly into a backpack).

All this by way of saying that this drill works for swingers and for those of an indoors or out-of-doors bent, as well as working for people whose tastes fall between these extremes. This drill, please note, is not confined necessarily to wives, husbands, or lovers. It works as well with business partners, old drinking buddies, or anyone with whom a relationship is deteriorating.

The following drill cleans up any areas of personal funkiness within a special relationship like a marriage ("We've been married four years, and he doesn't care what I do around the house, and I'm bored to death with his work") or a business partnership where two people work together nine to five for a mutually profitable goal, but couldn't care less what the other does once the lights are out in the shop and the burglar alarm turned on. And it does wonders on the sort of relationship where "She's the Greatest Gal in the World" (and he loves her) and "He's the Greatest Guy in the World" (and she loves him), only their marriage is a bunch of bullshit.

> INSTRUCTIONS: Take a 3" x 5" card or a piece of paper, and, as before, write the following questions on it:
> 1. "What's not all right about our _____?"
>
> In the blank space, write the particularly appropriate description of your relationship: *hub-cap stealing ring; bookmaking operation; massage parlor;* etc.
> 2. "In relation to our _____, what failures have occurred?"
> 3. "In relation to our _____, what have you done that's not all right?"
> 4. "In relation to our _____, how have you failed?"
> 5. "In relation to our _____, what have I done that's not all right?"
> 6. "In relation to our _____, how have I failed?"

One partner reads off each of the above six questions, one by one.

Upon asking the first question, his partner answers it. The answer is acknowledged and the next question read off.

When all six questions have been asked, answered, and

acknowledged, the card changes hands, and these same six questions are now asked by the partner who had previously been answering them.

This process is followed until both partners are in a good place about their co-created specific relationship.

In this drill, you will possibly encounter a professional apologist in the form of your partner; someone who feels as though he has badly erred although he has in fact behaved adequately, if not admirably. Do *not* buy his *mea culpas* and true confessions; if he begins with them, merely acknowledge his answers without feeling compelled to point out his particular psychological quirk with a breezy "I'll bet every time someone runs a red light, you're on the phone to the desk sergeant down at the precinct confessing that you kidnapped Judge Crater." None of the drills in this chapter calls for any kind of psychological expertise on your part. Just ask the questions as they come up, listen to the answers patiently, and acknowledge them.

The drills in this chapter, together with some of the ones we'll be presenting in subsequent ones, are absolutely guaranteed to put your relationships in the most ideal condition imaginable. If you and your close personal terminal are currently sharing a slough of despond, you will—if you will stick to the rather rigid format of the drills we are providing—turn that swamp into a Land of Oz, the rock candy mountain being strictly optional.

A Closing Note

If for any good reason, you have tried the drills in this chapter and they have not worked for you (in about 3 to 5 percent of the readers this will be true), then have a go at the following drills which cover approximately the same psychospiritual terrain.

These questions can be added to (or can entirely supplant) any of the questions in the previous drills. They partake of the same format.

Working with Yourself

question a): "What have I done to _____?"
question b): "What have I withheld from _____?"

question c): "What has _____ done to me?"
question d): "What has _____ withheld from me?"

The efficiency of this drill is not always at its peak when run alone. It works better when you are working on it with a friendly third party, and it brings about virtual miracles when you and The Special Other are running it together—although often this last format brings up some very heavy emotions.

Working with a Partner

Your friend asks you the following four questions:
question a): "What have you done to _____ ?"
question b): "What have you withheld from _____ ?"
question c): "What has _____ done to you?"
question d): "What has _____ withheld from you?"

The entire area of withheld creativity is an important one because it covers those areas which the Catholic Church calls "Sins of Omission."

For example, a woman becomes angry with her boyfriend and neglects to tell him that the important phone call he's been anxiously awaiting came through while he was out buying cigarettes. She watches as he pines and frets all day long waiting for the phone to ring, withholding the information that she told the caller that he'd phone as soon as he returned from the store. Or a man withholds from his lady love the insignificant fact that he has a wife and kids in a tract house in West Covina—because he didn't want to ruin their perfect idyl. Such instances of tenderheartedness have been known to end with one partner screaming some cliché like—"All Women Are Treacherous Mata Haris!" or "Never Trust a Man. Never! Never! Never!"—before a blunt instrument or a .32 is brandished.

So it is good to get these withheld communications out into the open, if for no other reason than that they tend to fester inside you.

In this particular drill, the first two questions are the important ones; the second two do not always apply. If, after two or three times through this drill, you find that you're not getting much action off them, then forget them and concentrate on asking the first two questions over and over and over again.

Working with THE Terminal

Write these questions down on a card:
question a): "What have I done to you?"
question b): "What have I withheld from you?"
question c): "What have you done to me?"
question d): "What have you withheld from me?"

Ask these questions back and forth.

Note that frequently the "What have I withheld?" question draws a blank. It's okay to ask "What do you feel like I've withheld from you?" instead, or, if absolutely necessary, let your partner cop out on this one. (This question only.)

This is the greatest single mover, and remover, of negativity that you have run so far. By the time you successfully complete this drill, you and your special terminal (or just you alone) will be in shape to get into the really thorny areas where the deep emotions lie coiled, and the upsets and confusions feed off each other like maggots when they're not breeding like tsetse flies.

4

Standards Betrayed

The drills in this chapter are great subliminal calmer-downers in that they are out to remove old, impacted standards, the bulk of which lead to disillusion and bitterness.

"She told me how much getting married meant to her, so we went out and, little able to afford it, blew $1,200 on the wedding, and then when we got to the bridal suite, she passed out on me. . . ." "I'm really happy. He's my dream man. He's everything I've always wanted—but why doesn't he shave every day?" "My partner is terrific. Handles the personnel like a Solon; meets every payroll like J.P. O'Nassis, has the mind of a digital computer. Only how come he and that sexy redhead from the typing pool both left early Tuesday afternoon and neither one of them has been in the office for three days now?" "My dad was my hero. He was Bruce Lee and John Wayne and Joe DiMaggio all rolled into one, with a little bit of Stan Musial on the side. I can't believe he had underworld connections—when those two plainclothesmen came by our house with a warrant, I thought my heart would break! I've never gotten over that!" "I idolized my big sister. She brought me up; was like a mother to me. The day she dropped out of the 4-H club to elope with a soldier in the SLA was the day my childhood ended."

The drills in this chapter are out to heal old injuries and cauterize still flowing psychic wounds.

The reason we become disillusioned in our relations with others—or at least one of the major reasons—is because of the standards, and they are often subliminal ones, which we carry around with us at all times. Most of us enter into a relationship with a whole slew of expectations; the other whom we meet and fixate upon matches perhaps two of the ten standards we are projecting. On a subliminal level (*i.e.*, a partly conscious one) we make the following equation: WELL, HE (SHE) MATCHES TWO OF MY TEN REQUIREMENTS, I CAN SEE THAT. . . . I KNOW HE (SHE) POSSESSES THE EIGHT OTHER ONES IN AMPLE ABUNDANCE. Ergo "I adore you!" As time grinds on, and the fascinating other does not display all of the other eight expectations, we begin to feel betrayed. As in the wellspring of initial attraction, the feeling of betrayal begins on a totally unconscious or partly unconscious (*i.e.*, subliminal) level.

In illustration of this: "I want a girl 5'2" with eyes of blue. I dream about her, fantasize upon her, lust after her, long for her. Then I meet you. You who are 5'3" and your eyes are kind of gray-green . . . but that's close enough. Pouf! I'm in love with you. You've got everything I've always been desirous of. Only, as I get to know you better, I realize that you don't brush after every meal—but, darlin', that's okay. You're still perfect, even though you tease your hair and smoke cigarettes and have a voice like overstressed steel and your hands are clammy and you've got two kids by a former marriage who have the disposition of junior ax murderers . . . and all of a sudden I'm starting to hate you! How dare you not live up to my dreams! All you wanted to do was meet some guy who'd be a father figure to those brats of yours. You never really loved me!"

We are, needless to say, compressing a good deal of clock time into one paragraph, but we do this to chart the flow of a bitter disillusionment, because the preposterous male whom we have parodied in the above paragraph truly feels bitterly disillusioned. He is betrayed and—at least to that part of his mind that can't see a rose but for activating a dread of spiders—the betrayal is genuine. The feelings that this betrayal summons are, though unmerited, certainly genuine in their passionate intensity.

This is to say that to the I-love-roses part of your mind, which is that of conscious awareness, there is no betrayal; but to the there's-a-rose-but-those-goddamn-spiders-are-out-to-get-me part of your mind, the betrayal is as real as today's headlines. Viewing these "betrayals" in a systematic manner brings them up to the level of conscious awareness where they will disperse like early morning fog before the quickening rays of the sun. Most generally, a person who begins looking at his feelings of subliminal betrayal will react with great gobs of anger, the dramatization of which lends little to the serenity of the relationship. But, in a drill format, the anger or the hurt (or a combination of the two) can surface and safely discharge. Once the anger and the hurt have dissipated, along with the chain of betrayals, it then becomes infinitely more possible to share in a mutually rewarding, consciously co-created endeavor, like a marriage; a love affair; a partnership.

In short, *it becomes truly possible to love another.*

"I Love You" versus "I Love You Because"

"Love" is an inadequate term to describe the oneness of beings. On a human level, when one being loves another, it's beautiful, but when the human in question gets into a set of mechanical love behaviors (or mechanical affinities toward another)—"I love you because you're almost 5'2" with eyes of blue"—the going often gets rocky.

Just plain "I love you. Thank you for being" is the ground on which lasting relationships are nurtured and formed. But "I love you because . . . (you're Jewish; you're a Christian Scientist; you're a stockbroker; you're an airline stewardess; you've got red hair; your lips remind me of Raquel Welch's; you've got a physique like Jim Brown's)" is what fouls things up. The *because* (whatever it may qualify) is from an other than present-time (Right Here/Right Now) context and is the mechanical affinity, brought about by the Automatic Mind, that will invariably lead to nagging feelings of betrayal. All of these millions of different betrayals can be described in the following formula: *"I'm mad as hell at you because you didn't match the pictures I had of you."* Now this is palpably absurd: A quick look at the last sentence will show anyone that the pictures in question were created by the subject of the sentence, the "I." The computation is not a rational one: I create pictures of how you ought to be (to match my perfect standard), and you continue being you (which is perfect), but I—I turn around and get mad at you! This would be called insanity if it weren't so universal a pattern of behavior.

("Sanity", my coauthor chuckles. "You know what sanity is? A socially approved aberration.")

The *because* in "I love you because . . ." is that small percentage of expectations, assumptions, and standards which more often than not make you decide that THIS is my soul-mate. He/She is THE ONE for me. "I want a strong, reverent, courteous, kind, good-providing husband. So I marry a 6'5" tightwad who begrudges me forty cents for the laundromat. . . ." Unfortunately, these *becauses* tend to be automatic and subliminal. Most generally, they come in matched sets. The filling of this great psychic order, even if it's only 10 percent equals the filling of the rest of this set. "I also expect him to be brave, considerate, clean, and moral. . . ." Odds are that in real life, the day-to-day living that follows the honeymoon, you can squeeze an additional 10 percent of your requirements out of him before he gets fed up.

Of course, in every likelihood, he is surrounded by similar pictures of what an ideal wife should be, and by the time he pushes you into the same bag ("The girl that I marry will have to be as loving as a nursing mother, as sexually inventive as a Thaïs, as uncomplaining as Red Ryder's sidekick, Little Beaver, as thrifty as a Grand'ma Yokum, as compassionate as Florence Nightingale"), you will both be doubly bent out of shape, and the hostilities between the two of you will be rife.

However, the remaining 60 to 90 percent stand out as screaming psychic betrayals, unknown, unacknowledged, and surfacing only as varying degrees of genuine incompatibility.

The following drill is the major cause of my coauthor's moving out of his last three apartments: The rooms became stacked so full of successful case histories there was no living space left. This drill can be run solo, with a friendly but unemotionally involved third party, or with THE terminal. Check your own life circumstances before deciding who your partner will be on this drill or if, indeed, there should be a partner at all.

If you are on very good speaking terms with THE terminal, run this drill with him or her.

If communication between the two of you is even to a slight degree inhibited, then this drill is best run with a third party instead of THE terminal and your terminal can find his or her own friend with whom to run this drill. (Overwhelming volumes of victories with this drill occur in this form. But the drill can also be run solo—i.e., you're running it on you—but, save for a very few instances, soloing on this drill is a very poor solution.)

With a Friend

Have your friend sit down opposite you, make good eye contact with you, and then ask for the name of the person whom you feel has betrayed your love, trust, sincere displays of affection, etc. Once this has been accomplished, have your friend ask you:

question a): "In relation to _____, what did you expect?"

Answer this question. Your friend acknowledges your answer, then asks you:

question b): "In relation to _____, what didn't you expect?"*

question c): "In relation to you, what do you assume _____ expected?"

question d): "In relation to you, what do you assume _____ did not expect?"

Explanation

Question a), "In relation to _____, what did you expect?",

---

*Just because we are not typing in the fact that you answer this question and have your answer acknowledged is no reason for you to assume that neither of these ensuing steps takes place. You should understand by now that the format of every drill in this book demands an answer and an acknowledgment.

works at first with obvious, surface standards. As it comes up again and again, as the entire drill is repeated, it digs into the subliminal legions of unmet and unconfronted ancient standards. Entire hordes of hungry spiders will be demobilized by this question answered and acknowledged repetitively.

Question *b)* when answered regularly and frequently pulls the same "sins" as question *a)*, but brings to light qualities unworthy of a terminal as great as my automatic realities have assumed you are. "I expected you to be great when I married you. I never expected you to pick your nose in public. . . ." This question will put a few more battalions of little crawlies back into their holes and will go far toward making the planet safe for roses.

Question *c)*, "In relation to you, what do you assume _____ expected?", gets into one of the more selfish and noncommunicative areas of your relationship with _____. Your assumptions of what another expects are not necessarily related to the actuality of the other's expectations. Your assumptions are presented to the other as dramatizations drawn upon *your* experience of how to please within the context of *your* concept of what pleasure is. If your intuitive feeling of how to please were in agreement with _____'s, then you'd be curled up loving _____ , and the two of you would be living and co-creating a joyful relationship instead of puzzling over the drills in this snide little book.

For instance: "You ate fourteen helpings of my roast beef last night and were so exhausted that you could scarcely pull yourself into the TV room to watch the Bob Hope Special before falling asleep. This indicated to me a severe lack of vitamins B, D, J, L, and trace minerals in your diet. And so, in order to please you, I've padlocked the oven and tonight I'm serving only raw cucumbers, unpeeled carrots, and whole grain bran bread. This and pure distilled water will be our diet henceforth. I'm just doing this for your sake, Archie. . . ."

Question *c)* calls to consciousness the automatic and assumptive dramatization and counterdramatizations of how to please the Him or Her that he or she would be if he or she were the He or She whom you have imagined him or her being.

Another big item that this particular question handles is the spurious invalidation of my best countercreations meant to please. For example: "I was only trying to make Archie happy by cutting rare meats and starches from his diet; I did my very best, but he just stormed out of the house to eat at a restaurant. I'm worthless and he's a bastard. Boohoo. Sobsob. Sniff. . . ." This unnecessary anger and invalidation are beautiful things to be without.

Question d) handles the same spider upside-down. "Archie would never expect me to cook the same meal twice. He had fourteen helpings the last time and needed an oxygen tent. I'm sure he never expects to see rare roast beef with platters of crisp Yorkshire pudding and schooners of gravy again." What you assume _____ did not expect is merely another withholding of the real you from the real him or her. You don't need this, either. Neither does he or she.

With THE Terminal

If you sincerely feel close enough to your special other to be able to run this drill without coming to blows, then the supereffective but touchy, direct, you-and-THE-terminal version which follows is fantastic:

1. Write the following questions on an index card or a piece of paper, legibly.

question a): "What have you expected of me?"
question b): "What have you not expected of me?"
question c): "What do you assume I've expected of you?"
question d): "What do you assume I did not expect of you?"

2. As mentioned before, but probably not forcibly enough, the asker of the questions sits down opposite the person who will answer them, makes good eye contact with him or her, reads aloud the first question, and then shuts up while his or her partner answers the question.

After the first question has been answered, the person asking it acknowledges receipt of his partner's answer with an "I got that" or an "I heard that" or a "Thank you"—and that's *all* he says!

No debate ensues. No tears. No grief. No elegies to a terminally wounded pride. Just a "Thank you for telling me that."

The person asking these questions, whom we will call the Asker, next moves on to question *b)* which he asks, and then awaits the Responder's reply silently and patiently. And so forth.

The person answering the question (the Responder) answers it as thoroughly and as honestly as he can. He does not dramatize, defend, or evade.

The Asker continues in his role as Asker until all four questions *(a)-(d)* have been asked, answered, and acknowledged. The roles are then changed, but the same drill format is adhered to.

These same four questions are asked back and forth until each partner feels that there is a realistic sharing of me-exactly-as-I-am flowing between him and his partner. (Until I know you're seeing me, and not your pictures of how I should be; and until I know I'm seeing you, and not my ideal version of you—or my tarnished ideal version of you.) Remember: Relationships come and go, but ideal standards are a joy forever.

Instructions for Running This Drill Solo

Soloing on the drill is perhaps to see it in its weakest form. The weakness can only be offset by deluges of honesty and vast numbers of repeated drill cycles. Working alone, these are the questions. Ask yourself:

question a): "What did I expect of _____?" Answer the question, acknowledge your answer.

question b): "What didn't I expect of _____?" Answer this question. Acknowledge it.

question c): "What did I assume _____ expected of me?" Answer. Acknowledgment.

question d): "What did I assume _____ did not expect of me?" Answer. Acknowledgment.

Note that no one is more qualified to ask you these questions than you yourself. But be aware of the fact that no one is more expert at deception, either. This drawback can be offset by a sincere desire to feel better, the ability to look long and hard at your assumptive universe, and the willingness to be honest.

To Clean Up This Area Thoroughly

Making a bearskin run is much easier once the grizzly is dead.

Standards Betrayed

The following drill should *only* be run once you have successfully completed its predecessor. If you and your THE terminal have gone to others to help you through the preceding drill, and you both are feeling much more in tune with each other's reality, now might be the time to try a little togetherness. Run this drill verbatim:

question a): "What *do* you assume I expect of you?"
question b): "What *do* you assume I *don't* expect of you?"
question c): "What *do* you expect of me?"
question d): "What *don't* you expect of me?"

If you don't feel lucky enough to attempt this drill on your special terminal (THE other), then have a friend run you through this drill:

question a): "What *do* you assume _____ expects of you?"
question b): "What *don't* you assume _____ expects of you?"
question c): "What *do* you expect of _____ ?"
question d): "What *don't* you expect of _____ ?"

This drill in this particular form is out to pave the way for future smooth-flowing relatedness.

Solo Version

question a): "What do I expect of _____ ?"
question b): "What don't I expect of _____?"
question c): "What do I assume _____ expects of me?"
question d): "What do I assume _____ does not expect of me?"

If you worked alone on the first version of this drill, be sure to run this alternate version, too.

In Summary

Now that you're in communication, shame, blame, regret, name-calling, etc., are no longer real possibilities (the spider and its web have been swept from the front door). You are thus ready to probe the more persisting and deeper strata of your nonloving creativities.

5

Eradicating Standards

The drills in Chapter Four were out to handle those last few fights you have had with _____ . The drills in this chapter are out to put you in a space where you need not have another fight with anyone else ever again.

Here, we tackle persistent standards. A rose is only a rose. To expect to see spiders crawling out from the convoluted swirls of each and every rose is (to coin a word) "mis-expecting." *Mis-expecting is invariably the result of mis-identifying.*

When you are totally aware of who or whatever is standing before you (Right Here/Right Now), then you are relating only to that person or to that object in present-time. Roses are too beautiful to shudder at, and you don't shudder unless you expect a spider. (Consciously, one sees a bedful of roses and no spiders; subliminally, one sees everything the rose represents.) Hence the following drill, simple to the point of tedium, cleans your roses up until it is only what it is. The drill also cleans shadow images and similarities that you have been relating to in place of your particular partner and/or object of this drill.

Solo Instructions

If you are working alone, you ask yourself this question:
a) "Who or what does _____ remind me of?"

Ask this question, answer it, and carefully list each and every who or what on a sheet of paper. The list can be only a few items or it can cover many pages of items, events, names, and faces, etc.

Making this list is done methodically and thoroughly until the name in the blank space provided is *totally* listed as to all he/she/it represents.

For Example

Let us say that I am running this drill alone. And I am striving powerfully to see Henrietta exactly and precisely as she is. I know that she has many chains of associations attached to her because sometimes, when I'm tired, I'll call her by the name of my ex-wife, Lucifera. And other times, during an intimate moment in bed, I'll start seeing Sally and Roberta and Norma and Raquel in my "mind's eye." Also, I've read enough psychology primers to know that my mom was domineering, and this "Either-My-Way-or-No-Way-at-All" is a trait I've often observed Henrietta displaying. In fact, the same bossiness that used to anger me when I was a child and my mother was always yapping away still bothers the hell out of me. And when Henrietta starts in on all my shortcomings, I feel a strong urge to stick my tongue out at her. . . .

Okay, so in order to bring myself into the immediate present vis-à-vis Henrietta, I would go to a quiet place, take out a piece of paper, and begin asking myself this question, listing each and every answer I make (and also acknowledging it):

1. "Who or what does Henrietta remind me of?"
   answer: "My mother. She was large in the can and quick with the tongue as well."
   acknowledgement: "Got that." And on the sheet of paper I write down 'My mother.'
2. "Who or what does Henrietta remind me of?"
   answer: "Miss Hitt, my third-grade homeroom teacher. She had a disposition like a basin, tub, and tile cleanser."
   acknowledgment: "Thank you." And on the sheet of paper I write Miss Hitt's name.

3. "Who or what does Henrietta remind me of?"
   answer: "Lucifera, who—although a blond—never had any fun at all."
   acknowledgment: "I got that." On the sheet of paper I list my ex-wife's name.
4. "So who or what does Henrietta remind me of?"
   answer: "A lap dog."
   acknowledgment: "All righty." And on the sheet of paper I write 'a lap dog. . . .'

When I am dead certain that I've got all the others I associate Henrietta with, I take the first name on my list (in the example given, "My mom"), and I give myself the following two commands:

b) "Notice something similar between <u>Henrietta</u> and <u>my mom</u>."

This I do. "They both have large asses and small minds." I acknowledge my answer: "Got that." Then I tell myself to:

c) "Notice something different between <u>Henrietta</u> and <u>my mom</u>."

This I do as well. "My mother is a widow, and Henrietta isn't, but would probably like to be." I acknowledge my answer: "Got that."

Then I return to command *b)* and I notice something similar between my mother and Henrietta. I acknowledge this answer. I next move on to command *c)* where I notice something different between Henrietta and mom; I acknowledge this answer too, and I return to command *b)*.

And I keep on alternately giving myself commands *b)* and *c)* until I can clearly differentiate between Henrietta and my mother.

Then and only then do I move to the next name on the list, which is that of Miss Hitt, my third-grade homeroom teacher who used to wield a ruler that way S.S. guards at Auschwitz did whips.

And I continue giving myself commands *b)* and *c)*, acknowledging each of my answers, until I can clearly see the uniqueness of both Miss Hitt and Henrietta.

Then I move on to the next name on the list: Lucifera, my first wife. And I do the same thing here. I notice something similar between Henrietta and Lucifera; I notice something different between Henrietta and Lucifera; and I acknowledge each and every answer I make.

. . . and this is the way the entire drill runs. I stick with it until I have consciously extricated good old Henrietta from a tangled skein of others whom she in some way—no matter how tangential—reminds me of, and I am seeing the HENRIETTA-NESS of Henrietta.

Running this Drill with a Friendly But Uninvolved Third Party

Your friend sits down with you, and makes good eye-contact with you. He then proceeds to ask you:
a) "Who or what does Henrietta remind you of?" over and over again. Each time you reply, he writes down the name of whomever or whatever Henrietta reminds you of.

When all the people and all the things Henrietta represents to you are listed, your friend then asks you to:
b) "Notice something similar between Henrietta and _____."

You do this. Your friend acknowledges you, and then tells you to:
c) "Notice something different between Henrietta and _____."

And you do this, and he acknowledges you, and then he returns to command b) and you notice something similar between Henrietta and _____; then on to command c) where you must notice something different between Henrietta and _____, and so the drill goes until you see exactly where _____ ends and Henrietta begins.

Your friend then tells you to do the same thing for the next name on your list.

You stay at this drill until Henrietta has clearly and completely emerged from the nexus of old associations that had been keeping this charming femme person from your steady and direct gaze.

Running this Drill with THE Terminal is slightly hazardous but ultimately rewarding, especially if both of you have done the rather heavy drill to which Chapter Four is mainly devoted.

Here, you sit down with Henrietta, and she asks you:
a) "Who or what do I remind you of?" You tell her (". . . foam-born Aphrodite, my dear . . .") and she writes down Aphrodite's

name and then asks you this same question over again. Note that after a while, your answers will usually tend to become more honest: My Mother . . . Miss Hitt . . . Sister Mary "Sonny" Liston . . . Totie Fields . . . Ilse Koch . . . Mizmoon Solstyk . . . San Quentin . . . etc.

And each name you reel off, she writes down, after acknowledging your answer. She does not begin to carp and sniff disdainfully and complain. She only acknowledges each and every answer you make.

When you are both quite sure that you have exhausted all the other people, things, and even places she reminds you of, Henrietta then tells you to:

b) "Notice something similar between <u>foam-born Aphrodite</u> and me."

You answer her. She merely acknowledges your answer and then instructs you to:

c) "Notice something different between <u>foam-born Aphrodite</u> and me."

You answer; she acknowledges your answer and returns to command b) and then c), staying with foam-born Aphrodite until you know with intuitive certainty that the goddess is the goddess and Henrietta is not the goddess.

Both of you then move on to the next name on the list. When you have exhausted every name on the list and are seeing Henrietta as she is, then comes the time for you to reverse roles. Now you ask her:

a) "Who or what do I remind you of?"

And now you acknowledge her answer and now you make a list for her . . . Attila the Hun . . . Grendel's father . . . King Kong . . . The Black Hole of Calcutta . . . Benedict Arnold, etc.—and no matter what she says, you do not wince; you do not flinch; you do not protest. You merely acknowledge having heard her communication, and you write the name down.

When you've gotten all the names in her personal lexicon, you then instruct her to:

b) "Notice something similar between me and Attila the Hun."

She does so; you acknowledge her, and then you tell her to:

c) "Notice something different between me and Attila the Hun."

And you keep on with this boring but vital little drill until she is seeing you as clearly as you are seeing her.

The reason why we ask you who or what _____ reminds you of is because if there are a whole string of others involved, then it is highly improbable that you and the real _____ have a real relationship going. There exists, in other words, a whole nexus of associations standing between you and Good Old Blank. If your relationship is to some degree alloyed by x-number of associations with others, then you are treating your rose to some degree the way you would treat a spider. We doubt whether this goes over any better with Rosie than it does with you. Hence we ask you to cover this drill thoroughly. (We well know that it can be and often is tediously repetitious, but hang in there. There is a pot of gold at the end of your list, and this prize is a newly acquired and permanent ability to see your spouse/lover/partner/associate instead of seeing him or her buried under a swarm of associational debris.

(When you can see someone who is close to you with utmost clarity, you can then decide whether or not to maintain a relationship with him or her. And if you do decide to maintain your relationship, it will change for the better.)

Standards Revisited: Or What Quarrel Have You Had with the Second Prettiest Rose in the World?

"George has really let me down!"

"Oh, that Henrietta! I just can't believe her! She's really betrayed me!"

Oh really? And what part of you did George or Henrietta "let down"? Evidently, it is that part of you that expected more of him (or her) than what, in fact, you got. What you got was other than what was expected. And what did you expect?

"Well, after all, I have my standards, you know."

Actually, nothing upsets you about the other person: He or she does not cause your upset. YOU MAKE YOURSELF UPSET, and the reason you are able to do this is because you carry around inside you ideal standards of what a husband/a wife/a parent/a child/a partner/a friend, has to match. If anyone close to you does in fact live up to about 10 percent of your standards (and assume that the other has; if not, he or she would not be close to you to begin with), whenever he or she fails to meet the other 90 percent of your standards—which are for the most part subliminal—then you are going to get angry with him or her. Count on it.

And this is the name of the game called Relationships: A certain (small) percentage of matched standards holding together a much larger percentage of unmatched or mismatched standards with all kinds of attendant creaks and groans as the entire edifice bends to remain viable under the terrific pressure your standards subject it to.

My coauthor and I have been fairly far into our own subliminal universes, and what we have found is that the one constant factor which survives any number of encounters with all sorts of creatures is standards. We have observed that most people tend to carry around within them perfect standards. Some of the more evident can be found in the following episodes from the soap-opera lives most of us lead:

> "Gee, I really like Paul. He's a super guy with a great physique, a terrific personality: He's warm, sensitive, loving, and he's working his way through med school. And he really loves me . . . if only he weren't black."

> or "Linda and I have been married for 500 years. Oh, I know, chronologically, we've only been man and wife for four years, but it's just getting worse and worse and worse. All our loving time is taken up by fights. At first, it was just one or two little habits of hers that bothered me, but now just about everything she does irritates me—and it's the same way with her: By her, I can't do anything right."

Just as roses tend to come and go, spiders persist. So, in any relationship, it is not the tender moments you and your lover share which endure, but rather the disagreements, the disharmonies, the discords.

(These standards which we carry about with us are literally murder):

> *for example:* "Rose has betrayed me with another man. Honor demands that I exact a blood vengeance!"

or: "That sonofabitch isn't leaving me high and dry for that bleached-blond floozie! I'm going to run through his checking account and wreck his car, and insist not only that I get custody of the kids but that he'll need a court order to be able to visit them! Nobody throws me aside like that and gets away with it!"

or: "I could really see our making a life together, Eric . . . but you're not Jewish!"

or: "Are you kidding? You're actually going to do business with a Cuban! Man, you're crazy—you can't trust Latins. They'll do you in every time. . . ."

or: "I can't ask her out. She's half-an-inch taller than I am. When she puts on clogs, forget it!"

or: "If my breasts were just larger, then maybe I could get someone to pay attention to me! Oh, I know I look like a *Vogue* model, but I'm flat! I must, I must, I must develop a bust! When push comes to shove, men only like knockers!"

or: "Soccer! Are you kidding! That's a sissy game. Any son of mine is gonna play Pop Warner football or else. I'm not raising any faggots in this household!"

or: "What d'you mean you're going to elope! Darling, every girl wants a real wedding!"

. . . and the beat goes on.

To compound our globally fractured relationships, many of our most cherished standards are not ours, but belong to others whom we admire. For instance: "My bowling team doesn't like my gal Sal" or "My ethnic group doesn't trust my business partner: He's one of THEM, and you know what THEY'RE like." So in the following drill, we are going to tackle standards not only head-on, but obliquely as well.

Run the following drill either solo or with a well-meaning, friendly, but ultimately disinterested other. This area is just too touchy for you to run with your Special Other. Have a friend ask you:

question a): "What problem of standards have you had with _____?"

question b): "What problem of standards has _____ had with you?"

question c): "In relation to _____ , what problem of standards have you had with yourself?"

question d): "In relation to you, what problem of standards has _____ had with himself or herself?"
question e): "In relation to _____ , what problem of standards have you had with another?"
question f): "In relation to _____ , what problem of standards has another had with you?"

Continue running this drill until the last "four years" of your marriage no longer seem like 500, and the long string of upsets you've had with your Special Other are so far into the forgive-and-forget bag that you have trouble remembering what it was you were going to forgive and forget.

If you are by yourself, grind through the following version of this drill repetitively. Ask yourself:
a) "What problem of standards have I had with _____?"
b) "What problem of standards has _____ had with me?"
c) "In relation to _____ , what problem of standards have I had with myself?"
d) "In relation to me, what problem of standards has _____ had with himself or herself?"
e) "In relation to _____ , what problem of standards have I had with another?"
f) "In relation to me, what problem of standards has _____ had with another?"*

Stay with this drill until you reach the space where you are truly willing to make a fresh start with _____ .

An Additional Standards Drill

The entire area of standards is so fiendishly complex that only a truly creative genius could have conceived it. Because of this standard/solution/problem vicious cycle, we heartily recommend the following drill.

Part One: Working with Another

Have an emotionally uninvolved friend deliver the following commands and questions in this sequence, repetitively:
a) "Tell me a problem of standards you have had with _____ ."

---

*Assume here that "another" can also mean "groups of others."

When the problem has been duly stated and acknowledged, your friend then asks you:
b) "How have you tried to solve that problem?"

You answer; your friend acknowledges your answer and then asks you:
c) "How else have you tried to solve that problem?"

You answer; you are acknowledged and then you are asked:
"How else have you tried to solve that problem?"

And your friend continues asking you for any other solutions you may have brought to bear on *that particular problem* ("How else have you tried to solve that problem? . . . Thank you. How else? . . . How else? . . . How else? . . .) until you have given him all the solutions you have pulled in to solve that problem.

Once you have gotten all the solutions to that particular problem off your chest, you will undoubtedly be struck by the following phenomenon: 'Here I am with one pound of problem and about sixteen tons of solutions.'

It is at this point that your friend asks you the following question:
d) "So what was the problem?"

Answer him. Tell your friend what the original problem was, and don't worry if you can't remember it or if it now appears to be of such little consequence that it is practically beneath your notice.

Part Two

Your friend then says to you:
e) "Tell me another problem of standards you've had with _____."

You answer him; he acknowledges you. Next he asks:
f) "How have you tried to solve that problem?"

You answer him; he acknowledges your answer and then asks you:
g) "How else have you tried to solve that problem?"

You answer him, and you are acknowledged, and he continues asking you "How else have you tried to solve that problem?" until you run out of all your solutions for that particular problem. At which point he asks you this question:
h) "So what was the problem?"

And he keeps on asking you this question until you are truly bored with that particular problem and in no way feel like going out and inventing any solutions to it whatever.

Then your friend asks you to tell him yet another problem of standards which you've had with _____ , and this entire drill is repeated until you have totally exhausted all the problems of standards that you've had with _____ .

Since the object of this drill is to bring you to a point where you can easily differentiate between _____ (let us call him "George" or her "Henrietta") and your standards and the solutions to his or her not meeting those standards, which have probably not worked, and any additional problems, we cannot let you go without your having a look at his or her other machinations:

Your friend fixes you with a steady gaze, and directs you to:
a) "Tell me a problem of standards _____ has had with you."
You answer. He acknowledges you and then asks:
b) "How has _____ tried to solve that problem?"

Since, at a certain level, we are all so close to one another that there really are no secrets between us, your friend will not buy your blank stare and your *I* dunno.... Instead, he will acknowledge your very reasonable reluctance to share this bit of information with him and patiently pose the same question again, and he will keep on doing this until you tell him. If you need to invent an answer here, by all means do so.

Once you have told him how _____ has tried to solve his/her problem of standards with you, he acknowledges receipt of your answer and then asks:
c) "How else has _____ tried to solve that problem?"

And he continues to ask this question until you have given him all of _____'s undoubtedly ingenious solutions. Once you have answered all his "How elses?", and there are no other solutions left, he then asks you this overwhelming question:
d) "So what problem of standards has _____ had with you?"

And by the time you get here, that massive problem will in every likelihood be reduced to miniscule proportions, and may even be a laughing matter.

Same Drill: Solo Version

What we want to get across here is that standards is a very tough area and, this being so, working alone with your standards (those beautiful, prizewinning, cherished creations) is difficult but by no means impossible.

So give yourself this command verbatim:
a) "Identify a problem of standards you have had with _____."*

Answer this question. For example, 'Well, dad wanted me to be a basketball player in the N.B.A., but I always wanted to be an accountant....'

Acknowledge your answer. 'Thank you.'
Ask yourself the following question:
b) "How have you tried to solve this problem?"

Answer it: 'I started smoking to stunt my growth, and took to hanging around malt shops with other, aspiring CPA's....'

Acknowledge your answer: 'All right, I got that,' and ask yourself the next question:
c) "How else have you tried to solve this problem?"

Answer this question truthfully: 'I took to cutting basketball practice so I could attend a fascinating course in Tax Shelters.'

Acknowledge your answer and continue asking yourself question c):

"How else have you tried to solve this problem?" "How else...?" "How else...?" "How else...?" "How else...?", etc.,

until you have gotten all the solutions your steel-trap-like mind could and did devise, and once you have, then answer question
d) "So what was the problem?"

Answer this question; acknowledge your answer. If need be, continue asking question d) and answering it until the original or presenting problem is but a freckle on the taut skin of your body-mind continuum.

Part Two: Solo

Again, we stress that it is your *methodical* sorting through of all the solutions that brings you to a space where you can see the problem in its true perspective and in its actual proportions.

The other side of the solo version of this drill goes like this:

---

*If you dislike addressing yourself in the second person, "Identify a problem of standards I have had with _____." is fine for this drill only as far as we're concerned. We want you to handle your standards; the standards of a grammarian are not ours.

Eradicating Standards

a) "Identify a problem of standards _____ has had with you."*
b) "How has _____ tried to solve this problem?"
c) "How else has _____ tried to solve this problem?" . . . "How else?" . . . "How else?", etc.
d) "So what was the problem?"

Most of our major and pressing problems being composed of about 90 percent solutions that should have worked but didn't, this drill, when run with patience and honesty, will eventually be the vehicle for producing in you a mild feeling of euphoria . . . and a deep feeling of relief. DO THIS DRILL!

Back in the nineteenth century, the Cherokee Indians numbered among them braves who actually survived bullet wounds in the abdominal areas of the body, provided the bullet had passed clean through the body. The way they did this was to heat a ramrod until it glowed white and then to pass that ramrod through the body exactly following the path of the bullet. It worked, but it was pretty painful. This drill is like a psychic cauterization. Thus we have not included our usual "You to Your Special Terminal and Vice Versa" version—because here the temptation for one partner to begin laughing at the other's standards (and all hell inevitably breaking loose shortly thereafter) is simply too great. "You actually mean that my habit of paring my toenails each night before retiring *bothers* you! Why, that's the silliest thing I ever heard—Henrietta! Put down that butcher knife! We're just doing a drill, Henrietta! It's only a drill! You're not supposed to—I'm sorry I laughed . . ."

If you do attempt this drill à *deux*, bend over backwards merely to acknowledge your partner's answer.

"Thank you."
"I got that."
"All right."

---

*Or: "Identify a problem of standards _____ has had with me"—whichever version you prefer.

That's all you say. You do not smirk. You do not evaluate. You do not call your special other's standards dumb or childish or ridiculous. Them's fightin' words, pardner.

6

Acknowledgment and Creative Upsets

Communications is a flow and a creation. "Hello," say I to you. "How are you?" I have created a greeting and I flow it outward to you. "Why, I am just fine, thank you," you say in acknowledgment, and I understand very clearly that you have heard my flow and have received it. "Good," I say, and we continue on our merry ways.

This is an example of a complete communications cycle. I have flowed out to you, you have gotten my communication, and you have let me know that you have indeed gotten it by answering me. This is all that need pass between us, and you can go on unimpeded to think about whatever it is you think about, and I can go on to other creations. But . . . suppose another little scenario takes place. I see you. "Hi, how ya' doin'?" I say . . . *only you don't answer.* My communications flow is left hanging out there in space, and invariably I will start to get bothered by the fact that you didn't acknowledge my existence.

Instead of jauntily continuing on my way, my attention will start to be stopped (so to speak) by your not answering me. I have been unacknowledged, 'What's the matter with him? He too good for me or something? Is he ignoring me? Doesn't he like me? Didn't he get what I said? I don't really give a particular damn how that so and so is, I was just greeting him in a socially approved, conventional manner. Boy, If I ever get a chance to do him a disservice I sure as hell will. No. Now wait a minute: He probably just didn't hear me, the deaf jerk. Dumb, too . . .'

We go into this little paranoid scenario in such detail because acknowledgments are of paramount importance in each of our relationships. We harp on this because there can be no communications flow between two terminals without acknowledgment. There is something in us—perhaps the desire for what the Gestalt psychologists have termed "closure"—that demands that each cycle we undertake—action cycle or communications cycle—have a beginning, a middle, and an end. To state the obvious: There can be no end without a middle. There is also something at work within us that gets very upset when a cycle is left hanging uncompleted.

ME (to my son who is watching "The Flintstones" on TV): Honey, I'm going out now. Please be sure to lock the door after me. (I start walking down the hall.)
MY SON (to me): ("   ") He didn't acknowledge me! Christ, has he become another of those glued-to-the-tube morons? My own son? What is he going to be, a high school dropout?
ME (to my son): Hey! I'm on my way out now. Lock the door after I go. Okay?
MY SON (to me): ("   ")

Whereupon I storm back into the living room, slam the knob on the TV dead, and launch into a tirade of when-I-talk-to-you-young-man-you-better-listen-or-else.

And as a result, my blood pressure goes up and he gets hurt and scared and has yet another reason for thinking what a dumb-jerk father he's got. The generation gap widens by another few centimeters.

The completed cycles, we can forget about; the incomplete cycles linger on indefinitely. Subliminally, each time we are on the short end of a communications cycle, all the other times that happened automatically come back to haunt us.

Incomplete cycles usually mean failures as well, and so all the past failures we have ever had will come storming in on us, too. And (witness me with my son) anger is usually not too far behind.

Communicate . . . or Else!

On this planet, acknowledgments are in severe scarcity. A waitress in a hash house sets a cup of coffee down before you—this is a nonverbal communication: If you do not acknowledge it with a *thank you* or even a smile—just some indication that, by God, yes! You get that she exists—she will come to feel that much more unacknowledged, unappreciated, unimportant, and embittered. She will also have that much more of a compulsion to relate the incident to anyone who'll listen to her version of her life's story whenever she gets a couple of drinks inside her. Now, at a certain level, she knows that she's boring her interlocutor, but she doesn't care: She has *got* to get the pictures of her life and its living off her chest. Every morning she serves 200 cups of coffee, and every morning she receives (let us estimate) 55 non-acknowledgments. By week's end she has 275 non-acknowledgments hanging her up. Two-hundred and seventy-five times she has been made to feel superfluous. So when she gets home and starts telling her husband about the white sale that's going on at Savmore, he had better indicate to her that he is hearing what she's saying or an emotional conflagration may well consume the two of them. Now, this does not mean that he has to express interest in the sale, but at least he had better let her know that her message is being received, because if he doesn't that's going to make 276 non-acknowledgments.

For his part, he may put in eight hours a day on the type of assembly line where if the foreman speaks to you it's to chew you out: "C'mon, c'mon, let's go. Get the load out! Don't goof off" If this is so, then there will be in him a hunger equally as sharp to prove to someone else that he exists. Thus he may show a marked propensity for going on endlessly about his bowling score. She couldn't care less about it, but she had better acknowledge the fact that he's talking to her or there is going to be trouble. All she has to say is "Okay. I got that." That's really all he wants. All he has to say is, "Sounds like a big sale at Savmore." That's all she wants. Of course, an "Oh really?" or a "That's nice," or even a "No kidding" never hurt.

If we would just get our acknowledgments straight, then the hunger for communications which we all experience would abate, as would the classical lament of the unrequited communicator: NOBODY UNDERSTANDS ME!

Special Acknowledgments for Special People

"What a day. Jee-sus. Nobody knows I'm alive. I've had a horrible day, baby. . . ."

"You think picking up after the kids and shopping and cooking your meals is any treat? Don't tell *me* about your lousy day—at least you're out in the world doing something! I'm just underpaid help here, plus I'm supposed to put out, too!"

This kind of interchange may win much admiration at a feminist rap session psychodrama, but it also has the effect of breaking up many a marriage. And the reason why this hackneyed bit of dialogue is so devastating is simply this: Each one of us has a special communications terminal, one Special Other whom we count on for acknowledgment. So what if nobody on the bus smiles at me? So what if I am but one of 7,000 employees at First Calvary National Manufacturers Guarantee Mortgage? *I've got you, babe.* I can always come home to you and be assured of the fact that my existence on this planet of 4.5 billion other species-members *means* something. Without your acknowledgment, who am I?

So if you greet me at the door with curlers in your hair and those three-sizes too large pink Orlon fluffy slippers on your feet and an equally pink, equally misshapen housecoat on (the kind the Chinese People's Army might look good in) and if you implement that greeting with Article Nine of The S.C.U.M. Manifesto (. . . if it's male, regale . . .), I will find a means of getting an acknowledgment out of you if it kills the both of us! Which it just might.

This brings us into the area of Negative Acknowledgments, which are the staples of all sitcoms. "I've had a lousy day. *You're* coming on like Jull Johnston.* I'm gonna show you! I'm gonna get drunk and wreck this place, and then by Jesus you're gonna have to acknowledge my existence!" Or, if this be too severe an example, there is the classic tableau from married life of her slaving away at the stove while he reads the paper. Every single cottonpicking day, he reads the papers. "I'm gonna make him notice me. Monday, I'll burn the toast. And if that doesn't work, Tuesday I'll spill coffee in his lap. And if that doesn't work, Wednesday, I'll set fire to the paper. . . ." and so forth and so on.

The drills in this chapter are out to clean up those areas of the pending special acknowledgment from that one special person and also those areas of casually negative communications which might be summed up by the following bits of dialogue:

> I see you. "Good morning," I say. "What's good about it?" you say. *or* I hand you a rose, and you spit on me (How the hell was I supposed to know that, subliminally, you equate roses with spiders?). *or* "Miss, haven't we met before? Wasn't it Antibes or perhaps Palm Springs?" "Fuck off."

In addition, the drills in this chapter also tackle the area of Stuck Acknowledgments. "When I review the troops, I bark and growl, and that sure gets their attention! How come Henrietta just gets sore when I confront her with my best barracks room style? Hell, the only way I know how to get some response out of people is by ranting and raving . . . only it doesn't work with her".)

Version One: Working with a Partner

This is the easiest version of this drill to run. A friend of yours asks you the following ten questions over and over—and acknowledges each and every answer—until you really and truly feel acknowledged.

a) "What about _____ have you acknowledged?"
b) "What about you has _____ acknowledged?"
c) "What about _____ have you not acknowledged?"
d) "What about you has _____ not acknowledged?"
e) "What about _____ are you acknowledging?"

---

*Author of *Lesbian Nation*.

f) "What about you is _____ acknowledging?"
g) "What about _____ are you not acknowledging?"
h) "What about you is _____ not acknowledging?"
i) "What about _____ will you acknowledge?"
j) "What about you will _____ acknowledge?"

This drill is by no means confined to human terminals. It works equally as well on "soul-less corporations" for which you drearily drudge year-in and year-out or on that university that treats you like just another coded Univac card.

Solo Version

Ask yourself these questions, one after the other, in this exact order, and be sure to acknowledge every answer you make.
a) "What about (the name of my special other) have I acknowledged?"
b) "What about me has _____ acknowledged?"
c) "What about _____ have I not acknowledged?"
d) "What about me has _____ not acknowledged?"
e) "What about _____ am I acknowledging?"
f) "What about me is _____ acknowledging?"
g) "What about _____ am I not acknowledging?"
h) "What about me is _____ not acknowledging?"
i) "What about _____ will I acknowledge?"
j) "What about me will _____ acknowledge?"

Run these ten questions through, repetitively until you *know* you are acknowledged.

Version of this Drill with THE Special Other

This drill works beautifully when run between you and *that* other person. Take a piece of paper and write down these ten questions in this exact sequence:
a) "What about you have I acknowledged?"
b) "What about me have you acknowledged?"
c) "What about you have I not acknowledged?"
d) "What about me have you not acknowledged?"
e) "What about you am I acknowledging?"
f) "What about me are you acknowledging?"
g) "What about you am I not acknowledging?"
h) "What about me are you not acknowledging?"
i) "What about you will I acknowledge?"
j) "What about me will you acknowledge?"

Once these questions are written down, decide which of you will ask them and which of you will answer them, first. Don't waste a lot of time choosing roles. Flip a coin, if need be.

One partner will read off each of these questions, one at a time, and will patiently await his partner's answer. When the answer is forthcoming, the partner asking the questions will acknowledge the hell out of the answer!

Then the partner asking the questions will move onto the next question, deliver it, await its reply, and *acknowledge* this reply. Then switch roles and continue cycling through this drill until both of you feel truly acknowledged . . . and perhaps even appreciated. The final two questions on this drill go far toward building a mutually shared future for both of you.

Once you get enough of this drill under your belt, you become absolved from a large amount of that most human of all compulsions, which is: I'LL SHOW YOU or I'LL SHOW THEM.

. . . They laughed at me when I sat down to play the piano. Blind fools. Now we'll see who laughs last. I've wired the stage at Carnegie Hall. The first time an E major is struck, my infernal device goes off. . . .

Which is by way of saying that a lot of the world's certifiable crazies got to a point of acting out their craziness by never getting acknowledged.

Run one form of this drill or another until you blow off most of the accessible emotional charge surrounding the entire business of acknowledgments.

Creative Upsets

My coauthor and I have a problem. Standards. Standards are bastards, and the influence they are exerting right now over your life, gentle reader, is quite literally unbelievable. This book is designed to reach as wide an audience as possible, and to communicate with that audience. If we were to begin telling you about what standards actually are and how they work, about 90 percent of you would dismiss us as science-fiction hacks. So we're not going to get into this area here. Before the average reader is able to suspend a very reasonable disbelief about standards, he had best have successfully completed the enlightenment drills which our book *Mind Games* offers. Only if he has these drills out of the way can that reader be ready for the really heavy standards-handling drills.

We're telling you this to convey to you, at least superficially, the extent to which standards run our lives. The drills in the remainder of this chapter are designed to have you begin creating on a conscious and volitional level that which you do unconsciously and untillingly.

The secret here is quite simple: The most effective way to cure some involuntary and automatic activity (like, say, hiccups) is to assume conscious control over the automaticity. Thus, if you ever "get the hiccups" and you don't feel like waiting until they subside, begin hiccuping voluntarily. In other words, consciously create hiccups. Start hiccuping. Hic . . . hic . . . hic . . . hic, etc. Assume control of this involuntary function and you will find that in a relatively brief period of time, the involuntary process and need to hiccup will vanish. You will have reassumed your rightful place, which is that of being in control of and over your body.

Much of yoga is based on this principle. Doing *assanas* a person arrives at a space where he or she can control every involuntary automaticity in his or her body—which can be a very fine space to occupy. On the other hand, you must remember to keep instructing your heart to beat and your hormones to circulate, but for those of you who are up to this responsibility, total control over the body can be fun.

Now, if you can do this with your bodily processes (*i.e.*, assume conscious control over them), then surely you can do the same thing with your mental processes.

Prove this by taking an active part in the following standards-stabbing drill.

The Drill Run with a Partner

Have your friend give you the following commands in this sequence, one at a time, and repetitively.

command a): "Create a mental image of that special other whose behavior is straining the bonds of your relationship with him or her. Tell me when you have done this."

Good. Now it is up to you to create mentally a nice "solid" picture of that special person who is giving you a hard time. Once

Acknowledgment and Creative Upsets 65

you have done so, indicate that this command has been obeyed.

Your friend acknowledges you. He then tells you to *command b):* "Get the idea of deciding how _____ ought to be. Tell me when you have done this." All right. Mentally picture _____ behaving the way you think he or she ought to behave. Make that picture as solid as you can—for instance, there's good old George enthusiastically painting the house instead of lying supine and comatose before the Game of the Week on TV, guzzling beer, and emitting herculean belches.

Once you have created the picture of _____ being the way he/she ought to be and behaving the way he/she ought to behave, tell your partner that you have obeyed this command.

Your partner will acknowledge you; he will then instruct you as follows.
command c): "Now get the idea of _____ not matching those pictures you have of him or her. Tell me when you have done this."

So—in your "mind's eye"—you now see good old George behaving the way he really does. Picture him snoring through the sermon at church and embarrassing you horribly, or see him bemoaning the fact that your mother is going to come visit you for a month this summer, or see him yelling about the bills you've run up. . . . Once this picture of George not meeting your standards is good and solid, tell your partner that you have obeyed command *c)*.

Your partner then acknowledges you. And he gives you the next command, which is
command d): "Okay. Now get the idea of your being really upset with _____ for not matching your pictures of him or her."

Do it. In your mind's eye, see yourself getting really angry with George for not living up to your standards.

Dramatize getting angry at him.

If you need to, get up and go over to a couch and, pretending that the soft pillow on it is George, begin pounding that pillow with your fists or yelling at it.

While you are engaged in this dramatization, your partner keeps quiet and merely observes you in high dudgeon and full fury.

Note that you do *not* have to get into a rage here, but if you do have suppressed angers at that low-down, two-faced, uncooperative George, by all means express them here.

If you have to cry, cry.
If you have to scream, scream.

The trick here is not to force yourself into a highly charged affective state. It is the conscious willingness to become upset with George that makes the drill so effective. The histrionics are just fun and games: little forays into hysteria.

But if you do "freak out" here, your partner should allow you this luxury.

Once your anger has subsided, your partner acknowledges you, and delivers the final command on the first cycle of this drill—

command e): "Cease creating these pictures. Tell me when you have done this."

And this is precisely what you do: You cease creating pictures of George and of your being upset with him. You inform your friend when you have ceased creating these pictures, he acknowledges you and then delivers command a) all over again.

Continue running this drill until you are totally in command of your ability to turn your anger at (George or Henrietta) on and off, and that the mere sight of that stingy tightwad (or that slovenly shrew) is not in itself sufficient cause for your being "angry at the world" for the rest of the day.

You will get to an emotional/psychological/spiritual space where you will be observing your body going through its highly complex biochemical changes when the anger "button" is pushed; and from that space you will tend to sit back and smile. "How cute: This body of mine really is into being upset. Ooh, look at those gastric juices percolate! Feel the accelerated heartbeat! Will you look at those veins stand out on this body's neck! My. My. My . . ."

This drill will go very far, if your friend runs you on it long enough, toward cleaning up all the emotional detritus left over from the quarrels which you and _____ have engaged in. But aside from blowing off the accumulated and unwanted bodily tension which is a residue of many and varied fights, its main benefit is blowing the automatic mental circuitry that the mere sight of _____ stimulates. In other words, you begin to assume control over those "gut-level" reactions so dear to the Humanistic Psychologists or those "feelings" the practitioners of Primal Therapy regard as so devastatingly important. *And you start to see yourself as the creator of your own upsets.* Once you get this on a deeper than intellectual level, you then have the possibility of true freedom.

Another drill that helps you attain this unparalleled point of view (wherein you see yourself as cause over the multitudinous mental and physical effects of your upsets) is the following one. We recommend your having your friend run you through it at least half-a-dozen times once you have successfully completed the previous drill.

Important Note

Do NOT run this drill or the one immediately preceding it with that one person in your life who is extra-special and who, hence, is the person with whom you have the most upsets! Instead, have a good friend (with whom you are not sleeping or investing your money) run you on these two drills. Or solo on them. We want you to accumulate a lot of psycho-emotional-spiritual victories in this book and to get to a place where you can have a winning relationship with _____. We do not want these drills to serve as a pretext for your compulsively ending what could possibly be a winning relationship with him or her. (*Compulsively* is the key word in the foregoing sentence.)

So when you have transcended a good deal of your automatic rage at George or Henrietta and can even start to laugh at some of the stimulus-response mechanisms which rage brings about, move on to the following drill, in which your partner instructs you as follows:

a) "Tell me an upset that you are free to create with _____."
b) "Thank you. Tell me an upset that you are free to continue to create with _____."
c) "All right, I got that. Tell me an upset that you are free to cease creating with _____."
d) "Okay. So tell me an upset that you are free to have _____ create with you."
e) "Thank you. Tell me an upset that you are free to continue to have _____ create with you."

f) "All righty. Tell me an upset that you are free to have ———— cease creating with you."

The drills in this book are rather carefully arranged along a sliding scale of increased difficulty and increased yield.

But please do not do these drills with your own particular George or Henrietta. Each of you choose your own friend and then, once you have divested yourselves of a lot of that burden of anger (which another's not living up to your standards automatically engenders) return to each other's company. When Henrietta is in a space where she can see George—the Georgeness of George—and George is in a space where he sees Henrietta for whom and for what she truly is whenever he looks at her, then they have a change of living happily together "forever and ever". Or they can decide that their union or partnership was a mutual mistake and they can terminate it amicably because the choice to do so will be freely theirs. There will, in other words, be no "injured parties," and the feeling of I FAILED (and its attendant blame and regret) will not be decisive factors in each of them resuming a life and a life-style in keeping—with each's wants and needs.

Togetherness Drills

"Henrietta, you know something: I really like you and I really love you now. It's this goddamn marriage that's hanging me up."

"George, I'll go out boozing with you any night of the week and I'll still play poker with you Tuesdays, but I'm blamed if I'm going to enter into this multi-billion dollar deal with you. . . ."

We have suddenly decided to round out this long chapter with a couple of drills aimed at cementing those ties that bind you to and with your Special Other: Your husband/your wife/your lover/your closest business associate.

Now the time has come for you and your closest personal terminal to sit down and experience each other's standards as regards your ———— (your marriage/affair/business dealings).

Your doing these next three drills is conditional upon each of you having completed the other drills. Note that, in many cases, industrious, hard-working you will have been willing to put in the time and the effort to complete the foregoing drills but that lazy-no-good husband (or wife or partner) of yours won't have bothered. Which is typical of him, right?

At least you will be able to acknowledge the fact that you have made an honest effort to get to a "good space" as regards your relationship. But instead of reveling in the glow of true moral superiority, merely see the not inconsiderable role you have played in sabotaging what up until now passed for a marriage or a partnership. In other words, don't gloat. And, also, give the other another chance. Run the next few drills with him or her—even if he or she hasn't bothered to read the pearls of wisdom in this book. As long as you're in a pretty good space as regards him (or her), then your relationship can conceivably not only continue but improve.

In the following three drills, though, it's important that you and your Special Other do them together. If necessary, each of you can bring in your own friend (the one who ran the earlier drills on you) to referee. But those friends have to understand that they do not take sides and that they do not make any clever or insightful or "helpful" remarks during the course of any of these drills. This is really the area of one-on-one . . . you and your tarnished dream man or you and your magic lady.

Sit down with Him or Her and decide which of you will begin asking the questions and which of you will begin by answering them. Again, if necessary, flip a coin.

question a): "What about our _____ (marriage/love relationship/business association—fill the blank with whatever term is appropriate, but don't for Chrissake tack on any adjectives like 'so-called marriage' or 'disastrous financial dealings!!') has been acknowledged?"

This question is answered honestly, and it is *not* commented upon—it is merely acknowledged with a "Thank you" or a "Got that" or an "Okay. I heard that." Then question b) is asked:

question b): "What about our _____ has not been acknowledged?"

And this question is answered honestly and it, too, is not commented upon, but merely acknowledged.

Now, hand your partner this book and have him read you question a). This is to say, immediately after these two questions have been asked, answered, and acknowledged, switch roles. If you started out asking the question, now you're going to answer it.

Let us say that George had asked Henrietta these two questions; now Henrietta asks them of George:

a) "What about our (marriage) has been acknowledged?"

George answers; Henrietta says, "Thank you for telling me that" in a level and expressionless tone of voice. Or "I got that."

Then Henrietta asks George:

b) "What about our (marriage) has not been acknowledged?" George answers truthfully, and Henrietta acknowledges him.

Then Henrietta hands the book back to George and he asks her question a): "What about our marriage has been acknowledged?" and Henrietta answers, and George acknowledges her.

Then George asks Henrietta question (b): "What about our marriage has not been acknowledged?"—and Henrietta answers and George acknowledges her, and he passes the book back to her and she asks him question a). . . .

The two of you continue cycling each other through these two questions—you will know where you are on this drill because whoever is holding the book is the Asker—until you both have gotten a lot of withheld gripes off your chest and the air between the two of you has cleared considerably.

Then move on to the next drill:

question a): "What about our _____ have YOU acknowledged?"

Response. Acknowledgment.

question b): "What about our _____ have YOU not acknowledged?"

And the same instructions prevail here. You keep on passing this book back and forth.

Continue running this drill until you have both gone very far in cracking what is one of the most insurmountable obstacles to the successful continuance of any relationship: that You-Ought-to-Know-What-I-Mean, Why-the-Hell-Don't-You(?) impasse. Naturally, this phenomenon has its roots in those "standards" we keep referring to.

Acknowledgment and Creative Upsets 71

A general description of this particularly disruptive phenomenon might go like this:

> He's my dream man and so naturally he knows each one of my dreams and desires (even the ones I'm kind of vague on myself); and if he doesn't, then plague take the s.o.b.

or

> She's my One and Only and so naturally she already knows all my secret fantasies and closet desires, and if she doesn't, then she's just like all the rest of those scheming females who butter you up before marriage and then, once the knot is tied, show themselves to be hussies.

Notice, please, that neither of the above two examples is in any way rational, but notice, too, that they are all the more powerful for lurking right at the threshold of conscious inspection. These semiconscious computations are the stuff that feeds so many of the sexist cliches both genders utter:

Men, they're all alike—you can't trust any of them;
Women will do anything to get some security;
Men are all lechers;
Women, they're all whores;
"Men—women, it'll never work." (Erica Jong)
"The man pays while the woman lays." (Jeanne Rejaunier)
Men (women) you can't live without them, and you can't live
  with them.

Now, there are many forms to this drill. For example, you might run it as follows:

a) "What about this _____ has been acknowledged?"
b) "What about this _____ has not been acknowledged?"
a') "What about this _____ have you acknowledged?"
b') "What about this _____ have you not acknowledged?"

Now, please believe us when we tell you that conceivably it can make a difference how this drill is run. "What about OUR marriage . . ." as opposed to "What about THIS marriage . . .," so if you have any reservations about this drill, it might be wiser to choose the more impersonal version, *i.e.*, "What about this marriage has been acknowledged?/What about this marriage has not been acknowledged?" etc. Run this drill and its offshoot in whatever manner makes you feel most comfortable.

When you and your dream man or you and your magic lady have cleaned up the areas of old unacknowledged needs and desires relating to your _____, then build some present-time enjoyment of it and some future for it:

Ask each other over and over again:
  a) "What about our _____ are you acknowledging?"
  b) "What about our _____ are you not acknowledging?"
  c) "What about our _____ will you acknowledge?"
  d) "What about our _____ will you not acknowledge?"

Or, if it feels better to you, run the drill thusly:
  a) "What about this _____ is being acknowledged?"
  b) "What about this _____ is not being acknowledged?"
  c) "What about this _____ are you acknowledging?"
  d) "What about this _____ are you not acknowledging?"
  e) "What about this _____ will you acknowledge?"
  f) "What about this _____ will you not acknowledge?"

"A Marriage Is Something Worth Working For"

By now, it should come as no surprise to you to learn that marriages are not made in heaven—although there's really no reason why they can't be. But my coauthor and I are operating on the premise that if you have had or still have the germ (or the husk) of a good relationship going with another person, then both of you might possibly be willing to work at its furtherance. It may be beneficial to your physical, emotional, and financial well-being to attempt to keep it operative.) So work at the above drill until it ceases to be work but becomes fun.

Then, just before boredom sets in (or just after you put the book down in favor of other games you and Your Special Other can play), run the last drill in this chapter verbatim and together.

> Before embarking on this drill, decide which of you will begin as Asker and Acknowledger and which of you will begin responding to the following four commands the first time through. Once you have chosen these roles, stick to them. Okay?

Acknowledgment and Creative Upsets

Good.

question a): "Get the idea of deciding how this *(Marriage/love affair/business partnership)* should be. Tell me when you've done so."

Response. Acknowledgment.

question b): "Now get the idea of *this* _____ not matching those pictures which you have of it. Tell me when you have done this."

Response. Acknowledgment.

question c): "Now get the idea of your being really upset with this _____ for its not matching your pictures of how it ideally should be. Indicate to me when you have done so."

Response. Acknowledgment.

question d): "Cease creating these pictures. Tell me when you have."

Response. Acknowledgment.

Then Henrietta passes this book to George and it is his turn to deliver the same four commands, one at a time, to her.

Since this is such a heavy area—there is nothing more powerful on this planet than standards—it is advisable for one of you to take the time to write all four of these commands on a piece of paper before embarking on the drill. The reason we are being so dogmatic here is because that Automatic Mind of yours is so literal. If that mind of yours hears a command like this:

"Get the idea of deciding how *a* marriage should be,"

your mind will, very obligingly, conjure up pictures of every marriage you have ever seen, participated in (even as a flower girl), heard of, read about, dreamt of, fantasised, or thought of.

Even the wording of this command:

"Get the idea of deciding how *our* marriage should be . . ."

will tend to have this same effect. And if reincarnation is at all real to you (increasingly, it is becoming real to larger and larger numbers of Americans), you might possibly start seeing pictures of you and "George" having been married before. Which is fine, but is rather beyond the province of this humble book. Here, we're out to improve *this* marriage (the one that is happening or that is not happening) right here/right now in the mid-1970s A.D.

7

A Final Thrust at Standards

This book, as we have said, is not planned to search out, attack, and destroy the very earliest or first standards from which all other ones gain their momentum. If you've done the drills for any length of time, you ought to be seeing your Special Other in a new light and appreciating him or her a good deal more. Still, you may prefer to let him or her go and hold onto your standards. This is okay, provided that the choice is yours and is freely made. Let's face it: The world is full of bodies—Georges and Henriettas come and go, but standards are perfection. They give us goals to aspire toward ("I'm going to change him for his own good"; "I like that girl; I'm going to make a lady out of her"; "What a fine person he'd be if only he had some religion in him"; "I could really go for her if she'd just enter analysis . . .") and security to fall back on when those goals are thwarted or totally undermined. Socrates will cheerfully sip his cup of hemlock because he's got his *daimon,* that little voice that never fails him and always tells him what's right. Socrates would rather give up his body than forsake his infallible right-ness. Joan of Arc has her standards, and she's perfectly willing to be burned at the stake rather than renounce them. Martin Luther King has a dream, and he's 100 percent willing to give up his life, and everything his personal life entails, to see that dream realized. In fact, what makes a person "great" may just possibly be the very visibility of his or her standards.

We have made this point before, but it does bear reiterating: Very very probably the person who is closest to you came to occupy that position in your life because you recognized the fantastic potential that other had to meet and match your standards. And when he or she failed to live up to them, you not only felt betrayed, but your entire *ethos,* your core reality, and your security (your entire knowing of how things work) was profoundly shaken.

In order to continue, you might then have decided to get rid of that other—no matter how much suffering your ridding your life of him or her entailed.

Since this computation is so closely connected to your survival, far be it from my coauthor or me to disparage your choice of action. George is just a man; Henrietta is merely a woman.... but MY standard is eternal, and my existence and my continuance are in large part built around it. It is perfect.

So what we would like to get across in this brief chapter is simply this: If you can at least begin dimly to apprehend the awesome power standards exert over your life and its living, you will be to that extent more free.

The following drill sums up all we are prepared to say about standards for the time being.

Ask yourself the following question, and answer it with utmost honesty:

"Now that I have done these standards drills in this book and am seeing _____ much more clearly, which would I rather have: my standards or (<u>"George"</u>/<u>"Henrietta"</u>)?"

Once you have answered this question, then make your choice.

If you would rather have your standards, then let old George go or permit Henrietta to fly the coop. At least you'll still have your Everything-That-Makes-Life worthwhile.

If, on the other hand, you decide that your standards are nice to have, but they won't keep your feet warm on cold winter

A Final Thrust at Standards

nights, and this being so, you'd rather keep good old George or sweet Henrietta, then by all means do so.

What this drill boils down to is simply this:

a) I would rather have _____ the way he or she is,

or

b) I would rather have my reasons for not having _____ the way he or she is.*

(Please be aware of one thing: Your close terminal _____ may be a drunk, an idiot, a painted lady, or a druggy, but he or she is *perfect*. Perfect in this case means far and away senior to value judgments like "nice" or "kind" or even "good" or "bad." George, for instance, can be a perfect tightwad and Henrietta a perfect scatterbrain. The point is that George is what George is, but the reasons you have for not wanting him derive their impact from the far-distant past. Your reasons, too, are perfect, but they do not stem from the here and the now. George is in present-time, or at least his body is; you reasons for not wanting George as he is are neither from present-time nor in it.)

Either choice you make here will be a winning one. But what truly makes your choice a winner is that it is *your choice*.

You have consciously and with as much freedom as is currently available to you, chosen a) or b). Do not spend a great deal of time agonizing over this decision and do not allow yourself to mourn b) if you have chosen a).

But we probably might add in closing that you are always* going to have your standards and that you will probably pull in another George or another Henrietta, the only unpredictable factor being the amount of waiting time.

---

*As a matter of fact, you could run this dichotomy as a drill. Take a) and start flowing the consideration that "I would rather have George the way he is" for two or three minutes straight. Then move on to b) and start flowing "I would rather have my reasons for not having George the way he is" for two or three minutes straight. If, after this time, you are still feeling indecisive about whether to keep George or dismiss him, return to a) and flow it some more; then flow proposition b) some more. Eventually, you'll reach the "right" decision.

*Or at least until the time when you are emotionally/psychologically/spiritually ready to start confronting the entire array of your standards—leading back to One Great Big One—on a gradient scale of increasing directness. The information which will enable you to do this will appear in the next several years in one of the sequels to this book that my coauthor and I plan to write.

8

Sharing Flows

Everything is flows and counter-flows, and everyone flows. Mental pictures are flows. Ideas are flows. Energies are flows. Desires are flows. Provided that the ideas, the mental pictures, the energies, and the desires pass between one communications terminal and another. "Hey, Tony," says my coauthor, "when we get this book done let's go fishing in Colorado." He is flowing the idea of this book, the picture of it being finished, the picture of a trout stream in the Rockies, and his desire of our flowing our bodies across several states to arrive at a space where trout flow their availability.

Now as long as his flow coincides with mine—"Hey, yeah! Let's do it! We'll really catch some big ones!" (Here, I am flowing my willingness back to him as well as my picture of a mess of sleek but plump rainbow trout), everything is hunky-dory; fine and dandy; smooth and serene. But if I say, "No way!" or "Fishing? Are you *kid*ding! You actually want me to deprive another creature on this planet of its flow of life? Never," then his flow of creativity comes to an abrupt halt. It has, in other words, been inhibited.

Each of us in his daily rounds encounters a number of inhibited flows. I get in my car to drive to the office and my progress is impeded by a whole bunch of motorcycle cops shepherding some politician to the airport. I arrive at the job and am about to eat a piece of danish pastry when my boss walks by and reminds me of all those inventory forms on the desk in front of me. I put aside my breakfast and start to reach for them when the phone rings! It's a customer wanting me to check to make sure he wasn't overcharged. I go to the file cabinet, but before I can pull out his duplicate sales slip, a secretary comes by and, with tears in her lovely eyes, tells me we've got a problem: She's pregnant. Upon receiving that flow, everything comes to a halt.

Most of us have had days like this. Recall how this counteractivity made you feel. At the very least, you probably felt frustrated. Those whom we are closest to we love the most, but we also tend to hate the most because they spend so much time enforcing their flows at the expense of ours.

Accordingly, the drills in this chapter are so structured that, if you take part in them, sooner or later those flows which you have initiated but which became stopped, impeded, inhibited, and which then became *hangups,* lose their identity as problems, and you as a personality and your life as your own creation become infinitely less stuck.

The first drill in this chapter is perhaps the most difficult. Try it out for size; if it doesn't begin yielding results for you after some five minutes, park it, and move on to the drills which follow. After you've done them, return to it.

Here is the drill. In this version, it can be run either solo or with a friendly but uninvolved other.

a) Define the verb "help" to your utter satisfaction. Consult a dictionary if need be. Once you have a stable definition in your mind, take the name of your closest personal terminal (your Special Other) and place it in the blank spaces provided.

b) Answer the following question in the exact sequence shown and get (or make) an acknowledgment for each answer:

1. "How could you help _____?"
2. "How could _____ help you?"

Sharing Flows 81

3. "How could you help yourself?"
4. "How could _____ help himself or herself?"
5. "How could _____ help another?"
6, "How could another help _____?"
7. "How could another help another?"

To answer each of these questions, you have to imagine (which is to say, create) a relationship close enough with _____ to have the answer seem real to you. If you run this drill long enough, you will inevitably begin to bridge the gaps that might still separate you from "George" or "Henrietta."

If you run this drill directly with *the* other person (your particular "George" or your special "Henrietta," whom you love madly but also manages so often to block your progress), the drill takes this form:

1. "How could I help you?"
2. "How could you help me?"
3. "How could you help yourself?"
4. "How could I help myself?"
5. "How could you help another?"
6. "How could another help you?"
7. "How could another help another?"

In this form of the drill, the "I" is the person who is asking the questions and acknowledging their answers, and the "you" is the person who is answering the questions. You and your partner should exchange roles after each complete drill cycle.

These questions are not all that tough, and anything less than a straight answer doesn't count. For example:

"How could I help you?"
Long pause; then: "You couldn't."
　This is a cop-out. Acknowledge it, and then continue asking the same question until your partner creates an answer.

Most of us are very unclear regarding help. Our version of it or need for it can range anywhere from, at one end of the spectrum, the states-righter who resents any flow of funds from the federal government to the manic-depressive who is always threatening suicide. This by way of saying that the questions are not all that tough, but the subject are ("help" in general) can be. So if you begin running this drill and you encounter agonizingly long lags between your asking a question and your partner's responding to it, then cycle him entirely through the drill at least once (it is, we repeat, important to complete any cycle you undertake), and then push on to the next drill. Eventually you'll return to *help* and look at it so often from so many angles that it becomes just another four-letter word.

But also note that when you and your Special Other are running this drill, it can get to be wild. For example, you ask him:

"How can I help you?"
He replies: "By taking me seriously."
"Got that," you say. "How can you help me?"
"By taking you seriously," he says.
'Thank you. How can you help yourself?"
"Uh, by, uh, taking myself seriously."
"All right; how can I help myself?"
"Same way," he says, "by taking yourself more seriously. People tend to walk all over you, you know."
"I heard that. How could you help another?"
"By taking them more seriously. Nobody gets enough respect."
"Okay. I got that. How could another help you?"
"I told you. By taking me seriously!"
"Thank you," you say. "So how could another help another?"
"You mean another person help another?" he asks.
This is not, you realize, an answer, so you say, very non-committally. "I get that you're unclear about the term 'another'. I'll repeat the question: How could another help another?"
"By the first another taking the second another seriously," your partner replies.

Now, obviously, what you've just gotten are seven slightly different versions of the same answer to seven very different questions. What this means is that your partner is very hung up on "help," and what it also means is that he is answering you from a whole entangled snare of automatic mental circuitry regarding *anything* to do with the term "help."

All of us have these circuits about certain subject areas. The best feeling I have ever experienced is what happens when one of these circuits "blows" and suddenly a whole blocked-off area of my conscious awareness opens up. If there be such a thing as a mental orgasm, this must surely be it! If you encounter such a mass of ensnarled circuitry in yourself or in your partner—and you'll be able to spot it immediately because all of your answers to these different questions will be monotonously similar (literally, you can't think of anything else to say)—by all means keep grinding away at this particular set of questions. Keep cycling the Responder because, eventually, that circuit will blow, and you will not only experience a delicious sensation in that fuse box commonly called the brain—*but your life will start improving to an undefinable but very real degree.*

Quite simply, what happens is this: When you become hung up on a particular problem area, your creativity towards it becomes blocked. To the extent that your imaginative, or creative (the two are synonymous), powers are frozen, your ability to project your other creations into the surrounding world becomes impaired. The quality of your life must needs suffer, and it seems as though the world is very stale and flat—a monochrome, casket-lining gray, no matter if the sun is shining after a night's cleansing rain. Stuck mental circuitry tends not only to take the flavor out of living, but also to inhibit your total ability to act and to react in the physical universe. Once you get those circuits flowing again, the world becomes a much more interesting place to inhabit. Enough stuck circuitry tends to push a person down toward apathy.

Probably much of the aging process ("Yuk! The alarm clock! Another shitty day I don't want any part of!") is accelerated by the total number of stuck circuits we are carrying around with us. By and large, kids have their circuits pretty much open and so, to them, each day is a discrete event with new discoveries to make and new adventures to enjoy. But as kids grow up into adults, the number of NOs!/STOPs/DON'Ts/CAN'Ts, etc., pile up, and more and more of their creative powers tend to become stagnant. It's a cumulative process. And a truly awful thing takes place: You reach a point where you can no longer imagine the circumstances of your life changing (O

84 RELATING

Christ! It'll *always* be this grim!") When this happens, you're in serious trouble. What imagination you still possess will then tend to go backwards into time-past or forwards into time-future because the here-and-the-now is so unbearable. When present time becomes unbearable, your options are greatly reduced. Eventually, you'll reach for that bottle of barbiturates and that other bottle of vodka or you'll have an accident involving your body and a bus or you can tacitly say to-hell-with-it-whatever-it-is and lapse into senility.

These drills are like spiritual isometrics whose ultimate aim is your enhanced freedom of thought and action which, as we have indicated before, are flows. They are also going to be very exhausting, and, for this reason, we advise you not to run any of them for more than two hours.

"Help" is the major one, but if it is too tough for you or your partner, put it aside and go onto the next drill. Which is:

1. "What problem could you be to <u>Henrietta</u>?"
2. "Thank you. I got that. What problem could <u>Henrietta</u> be to you?"
3. "Okay. I heard that. What problem could you be to yourself?"
4. "Thank you. What problem could <u>Henrietta</u> be to herself?"
5. "Got that. What problem could <u>Henrietta</u> be to another?"
6. "Thank you. What problem could another be to <u>Henrietta</u>?"
7. "All right. I heard that. What problem could another be to another?"

Problems, strangely enough, are easier for most Americans to look at and confront than the word "help." Run this drill through many times and look at problems from seven different points of view each time you cycle through the drill.

If you and your Henrietta are doing this drill together, its format is as follows:

What problem could I* be to you?
What problem could you be to me?
What problem could you be to yourself?
What problem could I be to myself?

---

*"I" is whoever is asking these questions and acknowledging "You's" answers.

Sharing Flows

What problem could you be to another?
What problem could another be to you?
What problem could another be to another?

"Problems" might be defined as "obstacles." Now, funnily enough, there are no obstacles in reality—obstacles become problems when we consider them as such and then when we fail to confront them with our utmost attention. But an obstacle is only a tool whose use we have yet failed to see; that's one of the insights which usually occur after this drill has been run for a sufficient length of time. (Dare we say it? Problems can even become fun things to have.... "Shhhh!" cautions my co-author, "don't tell 'em that. They'll think you're crazy." "And why not?" I reply insouciantly. "Craziness, and its cohort, sanity, are just two more totally created states.")

The next drill goes like this:

a) What solution could _____ be to you?
b) What solution could you be to _____?
c) What solution could you be to yourself?
d) What solution could _____ be to himself or herself?
e) What solution could _____ be to another?
f) What solution could another be to _____?
g) What solution could another be to another?

(I'm sorry. I goofed again. Before embarking upon this drill, be sure to get a definition of the word "solution" that is real to you. Have your partner do this, too.) The above version presupposes that you are working with a friend who likes you but who is not intimately involved with your trials and tribulations. Here is the version for that Special Other who shares your worldly victories and your cosmic pratfalls:

a) What solution could I be to you?
b) What solution could you be to me?
c) What solution could you be to yourself?
d) What solution could I be to myself?
e) What solution could you be to another?
f) What solution could another be to you?
g) What solution could another be to another?

A really strange phenomenon occurs once you start examining the field of solutions for any length of time. Not only do you begin to have a great deal of reality on our contention that "a problem is about 90 percent old solutions that should have worked, but didn't," but you will also start to see that solutions are so much fun that we usually go out and create problems in order to experience the joy of applying solutions to them.

For instance: The solution is *beefsteaks* (which really taste good), the problem is *I'm hungry*. The solution is orgasms, the problem is *I'm horny*. The solution is fame, glory, admiration, adulation, prize money, and advertising revenues; the problem is *winning the big race*. The solution is getting my way, the problem is *my yelling at you*.

Once this kind of "reverse logic" becomes ingrained in your patterns of living, you will get to a place where you do not automatically have to have an upset with Henrietta *when all you want to do is get your way*. A whole new area of getting your way (novel, creative, and interesting solutions) opens up to you and there will probably be a markedly more harmonious flow day-in/day-out between you and her. Problems are automatic solution-magnets. The more ingenious and unexpected solutions you are able to bring to a problem, the more you are going to enjoy having that problem.

"Speaking of problems, be sure to drop this pearl somewhere in this chapter," says my coauthor, kibitzing over my shoulder. "'Tis far worse to be without any problems than it is to be without any solutions."

"Gee, thanks, Mr. Wisdom!"

Games

Some people claim that the ultimate reality in this universe is games, and we are not about to argue with these free spirits. However, *games* don't always mean fun 'n games, do they? So before getting into this very heavy area, you and the person you're working with must each define the term "games." Get a

Sharing Flows 87

definition that you are completely comfortable with, and your partner should do this, too.*

Once you each have a definition of games that is real to you both, undertake this drill. We're giving, as always, the With-a-Disinterested-Third-Party version first.

a) "What game could you play with George?"
b) "Thank you for telling me that. What game could George play with you?"
c) "Got that. What game could you play with yourself?"
d) "Okay. What game could George play with himself?"
e) "Thank you. What game could George play with another?"
f) "I heard that. What game could another play with George?"
g) "Thank you. What game could another play with another?"

Eventually you will enjoy a great release from all the stopped-up circuitry that you have managed to accumulate around "games."

Remember those 1930s gangster movies: "Dish is no game, sweetha(h)t. We're goin fer all da ma(h)bles . . . see?" Remember all those NATO war games of the 1940s (and '50s and '60s and '70s? . . .) "the undisclosed nuclear device of a classified number of megatons was exploded last Thursday in our secret underground testing areas north of Las Vegas. The test was a qualified success whose results government scientists are currently still studying." Remember Eric Berne's best-selling books of the early 1960s and with what glee we used to go around "calling" each other for the games we detected and behaving as though there were some ultimate and God-given standard of High

---

*Note that, in this chapter, my coauthor and I are merely giving two versions of each drill, and are not writing in a solo version. This is because we're very sneaky. When you start running these drills with another, you and that other are going to get very close. You will thus create a winning relationship after awhile. However, if you are one of those strong silent John Wayne—Clint Eastwood types with a touch of the hermit in you, and you prefer your own company . . . but you still wouldn't mind getting to a space where you could have a relationship with someone else (on alternate Thursdays—if you really wanted to, that is), you can run any and all of these drills solo by mentally subdividing into an imaginary Asker and Acknowledger and a real Responder. Be willing to run the drills repetitively and don't worry about your possibly exacerbating any tendency to "schizophrenia" you might think you have.

Seriousness to which all thoughtful people had better adhere ... or else.... Remember those Top 20 love laments of the last 30 or 40 years which just about all of us have been force-fed?

> I wuz real sincere
> but now I'm stranglin on mah tears
> cause yu up an took yore lovin to town
> an I'm feelin so dreadfully down.
> See, I wuz all set ta give yu mah name
> but, tew yu, luv is only a game
> an all gals are the same.
> Saraleelou, Saraleelou,
> we all uv us are suckers fer yu.
> I know I thought yore hart wuz true
> an so did Bubba an Carl did, too.
> But we wuz wrong an yure the wun tew blame
> tew yu luv is merely a game ...,

etc, etc., *ad nauseam*. *Games,* dear reader, games. Who of us is lucky enough not to have a tremendous amount of fouled-up circuitry on this subject?

So run this drill until you come to see that there is *no way* any of us can avoid playing games and, this being so, we might as well enjoy the games we cannot help but play to our utmost. (It's really not whether you win or lose, but how much fun....)

The one-on-one version goes as follows:

a) What game could I play with you?
b) What game could you play with me?
c) What game could you play with yourself?
d) What game could I play with myself?
e) What game could you play with another?
f) What game could another play with you?
g) What game could another play with another?

Run this one until you and your Henrietta (or Saraleelou) or your George (or Ernest) are laughing all the way, and the both of you are truly perceiving that there's nothing wrong with games except not having any to play.

Sharing

What is sharing? Get a definition that's real to you, then tackle the following drill. Your partner asks you:

a) What game could you share with <u>Henrietta</u>?
b) What game could <u>Henrietta</u> share with you?
c) What game could <u>Henrietta</u> share with herself?
d) What game could you share with yourself?
e) What game could <u>Henrietta</u> share with another?
f) What game could another share with <u>Henrietta</u>?
g) What game could another share with another?

(If you are really feeling cocky, you might want to try this version: "What space could I share with Henrietta?" etc.—all the way through, all seven questions; then, "What time could I share with Henrietta?"—all the way through, all seven questions; then, "What energy could I share wih Henrietta?" etc.—all the way through, all seven questions; and, finally, "What matter could I share with Henrietta?"/"What matter could Henrietta share with me," etc. These questions when asked, answered, and acknowledged get you into some really wild areas. Provided you can have wildness, they can be a lot of fun.)

Another, apparently simpler but actually more difficult, version of this drill goes as follows:

a) What could you share with _____?
b) What could _____ share with you?
c) What could _____ share with himself or herself?
d) What could you share with yourself?
e) What could _____ share with another?
f) What could another share with _____?
g) What could another share with another?

If you are running this drill with Your Special Other, both of you define "sharing" and define "games" (gentle hint: Try to conceive of some area of human enterprise that doesn't have goals, penalties, and barriers . . . this may help you arrive at a stable definition of "games"). Then you run this drill on him or her all the way through one cycle; then he or she runs you all the way through this drill for one cycle, and you continue cycling each other through this drill until you both are willingly sharing great amounts of space/time/matter/and energy together.

    a) What game could I share with you?
    b) What game could you share with me?
    c) What game could you share with yourself?
    d) What game could I share with myself?
    e) What game could you share with another?
    f) What game could another share with you?
    g) What game could another share with another?

You could also run this "What could I share with you?"/"What could you share with me?" etc., but since games are everything and everything is games—as you will eventually see—it saves a little time to run the above version.

Since games are so universal, it almost goes without saying that this is a very heavy area of creativity right here. This drill can bring about tremendous attitudinal changes in you regarding the sweet mystery of life... or the sweet smell of success... or just plain toward life in general—because as those old circuits start unblocking, you start seeing the world through a wider and infinitely more interesting angle of vision.

Co-creations

You probably have a fairly good idea of what creations are, but what is a co-creation? The usage is rather specialized, so take some time arriving at a definition of this term that is real to you; your partner should do the same.

If you are working with a sympathetic-but-uninvolved friend, and you are still having trouble with your Special Other, this drill is run thusly. Your friend asks you:

    a) How could you co-create with <u>George</u>*?
    b) How could <u>George</u> co-create with you?
    c) How could you co-create with yourself?
    d) How could I co-create with myself?
    e) How could <u>George</u> co-create with another?

---

*George, you understand, is not present. There is just you and the person running you through this drill. At no time should any of these drills be run by more than two persons, though others can surely observe if they'll be quiet.

Sharing Flows

    f) How could another co-create with <u>George</u>?
    g) How could another co-create with <u>another</u>?

Have your friend cycle you through this drill until you have created a lot of co-creation for your Special Other to engage in. And if he is off in another room having this same drill run on him but placing your name in the blank spaces provided, then you are both going to wind up with a lot of mutually created space to frolic in. This drill does wonders for that nagging complaint "I can't breathe! She's always on my back!" or its flip side: "I can't ever get a moment to myself—he just won't leave me alone!"

Once you have created some psychic *lebensraum* for your One and Only, then have your friend run you on this slightly modified version of the same drill.

    a) What could you co-create with <u>George</u>?
    b) What could <u>George</u> co-create with you?
    c) What could <u>you</u> co-create with yourself?
    d) What could <u>George</u> co-create with himself?
    e) What could <u>George</u> co-create with another?
    f) What could another co-create with <u>George</u>?
    g) What could another co-create with <u>another</u>?

If you and your "George" are running this drill together, the questions are as follows:

    a) How could I co-create with you?
    b) How could you co-create with me?
    c) How could you co-create with yourself?
    d) How could I co-create with myself?
    e) How could you co-create with another?
    f) How could another co-create with you?
    g) How could another co-create with another?

This same format applies when the "what" is substituted for the "how." We probably should say something about the third and fourth questions in these drills for those of you who very prudently read through the text before deciding whether or not to take an active part in these drills:

> How could you co-create with yourself?
> and
> How could I co-create with myself?

look like very bizarre questions indeed. Let us acknowledge their bizarreness. Okay, consider it acknowledged. Once you start running these drills through a couple of times, some very strange phenomena will begin to occur. To summarize them baldly: The logical-positivistic side of your personality will begin to give way to a more "mystical" side. The logical, sequential side of your psychological make-up (THIS must follow THAT, q.e.d.), (this color is black; that color is white; each color is thus *either* black *or* white) has been acquired through education. It is a useful distinction that you have been taught, but this either/or type of thinking is not by a long shot the only kind that has validity . . . especially in areas dealing with that most mysterious entity called "self." A correlative phenomenon which may turn on to a marked degree for you is that of suddenly seeing your "self" less as a "George" or a "Henrietta" but as a being whose total sphere of operation ranges from at least the zero of body death annihilation to the infinity of personal (and even transpersonal) immortality with an attendant infinitude of creations and co-creations to have or to deny having. If you begin experiencing this, congratulations: You are on the threshold of enlightenment and an unbelievable amount of freedom is yours for the taking. The boundaries of the self, in other words, which might be expressed by the following classic sylogism:

> Caius (George/Henrietta) is a man (woman);
> All men (women) are mortal;
> Therefore Caius (George/Henrietta) is mortal

begin to disappear and you will start to see yourself or your "self" as it is.*

---

*If this does, in fact, happen to you, and you start to panic—the feeling being rather akin to the old bumper sticker: Help I'm a spirit trapped in a human body—we suggest your reading our book about enlightenment, called *Mind Games*, and running some of the drills in its penultimate chapter starting with Step Four.

To sum up: Even though the questions "How could I co-create with myself?" and "How could you co-create with yourself?" seem like nonsense to you (which is what they are: non-sense, i.e., they transcend the limitations of the five or maybe six senses which we have), do not allow their irrationality to hinder your answering them each time they come up in a particular drill's cycle. These questions point you toward the ineffable and the noumenal, about which—by definition—a finitely limited language descriptive of phenomena is and must always be inadequate. Enough said.

Care

What is "care"? Get a definition that is real to you before leaping headfirst into the next drill. Please be forewarned that a lot of us have a great deal of snarled-up circuitry about this term. I mean . . . after all . . . you're not your brother's keeper, are you?

a) How could you care about _____?
b) How could _____ care about you?
c) How could you care about yourself?
d) How could _____ care about himself or herself?
e) How could _____ care about another?*
f) How could another care about _____?
g) How could another care about another?

All of the drills in this chapter work on many different levels simultaneously. They are *processes* designed to bring you to a realization that you yourself are a process limited only by your own considerations of who and what you can be. Each time, then, that you answer a question like "How could (Henrietta) care for another?" you are forced to create, imaginatively,

---

*". . . that dirty rotten sonuvabitch! Don't make me laugh! All he cares about is himself. . . ." "Thank you for telling me that. I'll repeat the question: 'How could _____ care about another?" (Long pause.) "He couldn't." "Thank you for telling me that. Invent a way for _____ to care about another." "Why he's so coldblooded and me-first, he'd walk across the yard just to stomp on baby chickens!" "Thank you for telling me that. I will repeat the command: '*You* invent a way for _____ to care about another.' " "Well, he did send his ex-wife a picture of him in the nude for her birthday. I guess that's caring. . . ."

Sometimes the Asker has to be very patient and persevering to get an answer to this particular question.

a) Henrietta,
   b) another, and
   c) a certain amount of care.

Now, note this carefully: Each time you create a certain amount of care, you become *that much* more willing to HAVE care, and if you are willing to have it, you will inevitably become willing to flow care out to other inhabitants of the physical universe. It is when you are totally unwilling to have care that you become also unwilling to get anywhere near it, and that warm treacly little old heart of yours turns flinty and you become—whether you will it or not—a very solitary being. ("Oh let's not ask her to the party! She's so aloof . . ." or "He's such a sourpuss, he'd growl at us even for inviting him.")

This is thus a care-creating drill. Run it until you have created vast amounts of care. If you run this drill directly with your Special Other, here are how the questions go:

   a) How could I care about you?
   b) How could you care about me?
   c) How could you care about yourself?
   d) How could I care about myself?
   e) How could you care about another?
   f) How could another care about you?
   g) How could you care about yourself?

The drill works magnificently when you and He or She run it together and at good length.

Upsets

Define upset. Once you have a definition that is wholly real and serviceable to you, undertake the following drill:

   a) How could you upset _____?
   b) How could _____ upset you?
   c) How could you upset yourself?
   d) How could _____ upset himself or herself?
   e) How could _____ upset another?
   f) How could another upset _____?
   g) How could another upset another?

Since we spilled the beans on the last drill, we may as well follow suit here. Yes, you are creating upsets. No, you will not create them in order to pull them in on yourself. Why? Because you already have the upsets; otherwise you'd be doing something more fun than reading this book and doing its drills.

Everything in this universe revolves, from the point of view of a finite creature, around the question of *having*. Most people start off by not minding having someone else care about them and not minding having themselves care about others. Aha, but . . . heartbreaks occur. "I cared about Climactia and she left me for a producer of X-rated films! I'm never going to care about anyone else ever again!" Such a computation is fairly easily handled by a person's creating a great amount of care because, when all else is said and done, we don't mind having care. It's nice. A lot of us feel most alive when we are actively caring for another and, in turn, are being cared for back. However, upsets are another story.

Rare indeed is he who welcomes upsets. A person has to be chronically bored in order to greet upsets with very much delight. But we all have them. And since we do not all like having them, it takes a certain amount of energy for us to begin locating and identifying each and every one of the upsets. This drill makes us consciously do just this. After a while, whoever is being run on this drill will have to start consciously creating upsets to have with _____ . When that person is at that point, he will start feeling one hell of a lot better because he won't mind having upsets. Upsets will lose, in other words, their particularly obnoxious connotations and will be just one more type of phenomena to be found on this planet.

In addition, the person who is having this drill run on him will eventually come to see himself as the creator of his upsets—and this is a profound realization. I could, for instance, throw you into an arena with a bunch of hungry tigers, but if you did not agree that my act was upsetting to you, it wouldn't be. The universe you and I share is co-created, and I can pull a dirty trick on you only if you agree that what I have done is indeed a dirty trick. It is thus not too much to say that *I cannot upset you*—all I can do is spin my wheels; whether you get upset at my words or deeds is entirely up to you.

Run this drill until what we're saying makes sense to you on a deeper than intellectual level:

> So what if she gets drunk and stoned and starts painting a picture on the bathroom wall at one in the morning only she can't paint unless she has the record player on full blast, and you've got to get up early the next day to go to work? This does not mean that you have to be upset about her particular modes of self-expression.... But it also doesn't mean that you have to have this kind of behavior from your roommate, either. The door, as Epictetus the Stoic observed, is always open. You can always leave a relationship like this. But the state of mind in which you leave is entirely up to you.

This, in a nutshell, is what we're saying about upsets.

> So what if he wants to charge admission to a bunch of strangers to come in off the street and watch you take your bath? You do not have to get upset about this.... But you don't have to have this kind of carrying-on, either. Right?

If you run this drill with your Very Special Other, refrain from defending yourself and your actions when he or she is responding to the questions. Merely acknowledge his or her answers. *Acknowledgment*, once again, has nothing to do with *agreement*.

a) How could I upset you?
b) How could you upset me?
c) How could you upset yourself?
d) How could I upset myself?
e) How could you upset another?
f) How could another upset you?
g) How could another upset another?

By now, you should have the format of this drill down pretty clearly. However, just to make sure, we shall repeat the instructions:

First, you ask each of these questions of your "Henrietta" in exactly this order. After she has answered the first question, you acknowledge her answer—and you do not buy a story like (batting her eyelashes) "Oh, Georgieporgie, you could *never* upset me!" Stay with the question until you get an answer. Then, you and Henrietta trade places and she asks you these same seven questions, one at a time, acknowledging each answer you make. After a while spent looking at all the ways you have upset her and she has upset you, those upsets will lose a great amount of their awesome power to impede a free and easy relationship.

Surprise

The entire area of surprise is very, very heavy. "I was on my way to pick out my wedding dress when you called to tell me you had just joined the French Foreign Legion. . . ." Ouch! So before having a go at this drill, get a good definition of surprise. The following mini-drill might help you establish a definition that is real to you. Ask yourself, or have a friend ask you, the following two questions over and over again!

 a) What is surprise?
 b) What isn't surprise?

If you ever hesitate to open a telegram for a long moment, or if your pulse starts throbbing uncontrollably at 3 A.M. when the phone rings and your daughter is out with that perfectly nice young man she picked up hitchhiking, then rest assured that you are carrying around a fair amount of snarled-up circuitry about the theme of Surprise. If such is your case, we recommend your embarking upon the above mini-drill before tackling this one:

 a) How could you surprise _____?
 b) How could _____ surprise you?
 c) How could you surprise yourself?
 d) How could _____ surprise himself or herself?
 e) How could you surprise another?
 f) How could another surprise you?
 g) How could another surprise another?

Since great amounts of shock and grief are associated with the concept of surprise, and since they take a physical toll, you will often find that merely looking at the entire area of surprise corresponds with a commensurate feeling of new aliveness and alertness in your body. This becomes especially true when you run this drill with your Special Other (who each time you see her and it's snowing, you are reminded of how you felt when your mother up and ran off with that ski instructor; or who, each time he raises his voice to bawl out an employee, reminds you of your tyrannical father).

Very many of us are constantly carrying about an enormous burden of unresolved shock which impairs our ability to function optimally in present-time. This simple little drill blows off a lot of emotional charge still attached to those shocking incidents which you and your central nervous system were unwilling to have in the past and to which you devote large amounts of mental and physical energy resisting—even and especially to the point of amnesia.

> This really dreadful thing happened to me when I was three, and I went unconscious. I can't really remember what it was; in fact, I'm not sure it even happened to me at all, it's just that whenever I see a big black dog, my gut constricts, and my pupils dilate, and my hair stands on end, and I want to throw up. Only I don't know why. . . .

This drill will go far toward getting at that entire mass of old shocks and griefs.

Here are the questions that you and your Special Other can ask each other:

a) How could I surprise you?
b) How could you surprise me?
c) How could you surprise yourself?
d) How could I surprise myself?
e) How could you surprise another?
f) How could another surprise you?
g) How could another surprise another?

The direction this particular drill will head you in is backwards into time—way, way backwards, in fact. Since this is a book that deals principally with your relationships in the here and now, my coauthor has suggested our presenting you with an additional variation on this drill which you and your Special Other can run. It goes like this:

a) In this <u>marriage</u>, how have I interrupted you?
b) In this <u>marriage</u>, how have you interrupted me?

c) In this <u>marriage</u>, how have you interrupted yourself?
d) In this <u>marriage</u>, how have I interrupted myself?
e) In this <u>marriage</u>, how have you interrupted another?
f) In this <u>marriage</u>, how has another interrupted you?
g) In this <u>marriage</u>, how has another interrupted another?

You and your Special Other put in the term that most nearly describes your particular mutual arrangement. Note that this drill undercuts the immediately preceding one, for it is almost impossible to have a surprise without an attendant interruption of a thought or action-cycle. And a very common complaint in relationships that are wearing thin might be voiced as follows:

SHE: I was all set to graduate from college and become another Mary Wells, when he interrupted my plans by turning me into a housewife and mother.

HE: I was all set to join the Air Force and become a test pilot, when she got knocked up. And then she told me that it wasn't fair to Junior for me to do something as hazardous as fly experimental model planes, so out of deference to her, I've taken this job as a riveter at McDonnell-Douglas.

Interruptions are often viewed as truly hostile acts by one or both of the parties concerned. This being so, we advise your looking at them in some detail. The limiter we are putting on this drill, "In this <u>relationship</u> . . ." is there because it does limit a person's looking to the interrupting events that took place during the not always smooth course of the relationship itself.

Inhibitings

Interruptions are certainly part of inhibitions. But they do not make for the entire range of this term's sphere of action. So define "inhibit" right now, and once you have a good working definition of this verb, have a partner run the following drill on you:

a) How could you inhibit <u>George</u>?
b) How could <u>George</u> inhibit you?
c) How could you inhibit yourself?
d) How could <u>George</u> inhibit himself?
e) How could <u>George</u> inhibit another?

f) How could another inhibit <u>George</u>?
g) How could another inhibit another?

It's time to let another cognitive cat out of our bag. The net effect of your actively participating in the drills in this chapter (running problem areas that are really hot with a heavy emotional charge for you over and over and over) is for you to come to see that all the terms in this chapter—

> help
> problem
> solution
> game
> share
> co-create
> upset
> surprise
> inhibit
> betray
> trust
> enforce
> please
> fail to help
> responsible
> need

are created states. *And that you are their creator.* Another does not inhibit you, for example—the door is always open—*you* inhibit you, and then since you are not up to taking responsibility for the inhibitions you have created, you blame the lousy feeling you feel on that "another." Once you truly get this, you really start to feel free.

And only when you are starting to feel truly free does it become possible for you to enjoy *and to sustain* a winning relationship with another.

Because (and this is a hard nut to swallow and digest) in all probability if you do not feel free, your Special Other—your own "George"; your own "Henrietta"—becomes an only solution to your problem of inhibited freedom, and if you lose that Special Other, you go all to pieces.

(I know whereof I speak. I spent about three years in deep gray shadowy grief mourning my ex-wife. When she left me, I thought all I could do was die, and since I projected this unvoiced consideration which I had created so strongly, I very nearly did. I clung to her, in other words, because as a young man I was never up to having freedom. It terrified me ("freedom," Sartre has remarked, "is terror") because I equated freedom with emptiness. Ah, but She, she filled my existential void, and when she left, the void came in like a tidal wave and I went under. So I am going on my own experience when I suggest that your Special Other—the one whom you feel you cannot live without—has acquired this particular status because of your own reluctance to take responsibility for your own life and its living.)

The beauty of these drills is that they gradually bring you to a point where you see yourself at cause over your relationships. When we quote Epictetus and say, "The door is always open," the door in question need *not* lead to the soul's cemetery but to fresh fields in which you can frolic either alone or with somebody else. We will return to these landscapes when we get into looking at *need*.

The one-on-one version of this drill (you and "Henrietta" or you and "George" or you and your business partner or you and your teen-age kid) is as follows:

a) How could I inhibit you?
b) How could you inhibit me?
c) How could you inhibit yourself?
d) How could I inhibit myself?
e) How could you inhibit another?
f) How could another inhibit you?
g) How could another inhibit another?

Alternate cycles on this drill until each of you clearly sees that he/she is the source of his/her own inhibitions.

Betray

This drill goes right back to The Big Standard In The Sky, and if you run it long enough you will start amazing yourself at becoming violent about inanimate objects—people will no longer matter to you, but objects (like properties out of plane geometry) will become of passionate importance. If this starts to happen, drop this drill and wait until we publish another book that will show you how to handle such mental phenomena. It will probably not happen, however, especially if you run the drill in exactly the format we're going to present to you.

The reason betrayals are so devastating is that they derive their power from old standards around which a large portion of your so-called subconscious mind is constructed.

The following drill will get you fairly free on the extremely sensitive subject of betraying and betrayal.

Step One: Define betrayal. Your friendly but not emotionally involved partner should also define the term. When each of you has a definition that is real to him, tell your partner the name or names of those others who have really let you down.

Step Two: Your partner makes a list of these names. Starting with the first name on the list—let us say it is "George"—your partner asks you the following group of questions:

a) How could you betray <u>George</u>?
b) How could <u>George</u> betray you?
c) How could you betray yourself?
d) How could <u>George</u> betray himself?
e) How could <u>George</u> betray another?
f) How could another betray <u>George</u>?
g) How could another betray another?

Continue cycling through this drill on "George" until you feel pretty good about (a) him and (b) his wicked deeds toward you. ("But he said he'd always love me and look after me—he *prom*ised!")

Once George is handled, your friend consults the list and, taking the next name given, he places it in the blank spaces provided and runs the same drill on that person. He keeps on cycling you through this drill on that person until you feel okay about that person and his infamies. If there is another name on your list, your friend cycles you through on that third party as well. And so on.

Now some of us feel that we have had wretched lives and

that everybody we've ever trusted has done us in. Such people will tend to have a long list of betrayers and they could conceivably spend twelve or fifteen hours (or twenty or thirty) on this drill alone, which is perfectly okay. But as these drills tend to demand a certain amount of mental exertion, we do not recommend anyone spending more than two straight hours on one without a break.

The version to run when you are working with your Special Other is as follows:

One of you decides who will answer the questions and who will ask them and acknowledge the other's answers for the first drill cycle. When this has been ascertained, the Asker begins:

a) How could I betray you?
b) How could you betray me?
c) How could you betray yourself?
d) How could I betray myself?
e) How could you betray another?
f) How could another betray you?
g) How could another betray another?

Stick with this drill until both of you really get this cognition: *You cannot betray me, all you can do is make me feel as though my standard of excellence (which at one time or another you epitomized) has been dealt a fearsome blow . . . even though I am not quite sure what that standard is; at least I intuitively feel that it is right here, right on top of me.*

If you feel more comfortable limiting this drill to your specific relationship with your Special Other, add these words to each line of the drill. "In this (marriage), how could I betray you?"/"In this _____, how could you betray me?" etc.

Trust

What is it, *i.e.*, what does trust mean to you? Get a definition, then have a friend run you on the following drill. Use the same list of betrayers you compiled earlier. Taking the first name on the list, your friend asks you:

a) How could you trust _____?
b) How could _____ trust you?

c) How could you trust yourself?
d) How could _____ trust himself or herself?
e) How could _____ trust another?
f) How could another trust _____?
g) How could another trust another?

Each time you answer one of these questions, you are compelled to become "<u>George</u>" (or "Henrietta") for a moment. Each time you cycle through this drill, you become that other, and the amount of space you have created between yourself and "<u>George</u>" diminishes, for is this not in tacit fact exactly what happens once you decide: "<u>George</u> has hurt me and grieved me and wronged me, and I don't want to have anything to do with <u>George</u> anymore?" Are you not really saying, "I am going to create a great deal of time and space between <u>George</u> and me?" And is it too farfetched to say that there is also mass between the two of you (a mass of hurt or outrage) as well as a great amount of energy impacted in that mass? ("I hate that low-down, dirty doublecrosser. . . ." It takes a lot of energy to sustain a hate.) And are not all these four attributes of physicality standing between your flowing love and acceptance toward <u>George</u>?

When my coauthor and I tell you that the drills in this chapter establish and widen flows between you and a disliked or mistrusted other, we are perfectly serious. The drills also make you realize to what a fantastic extent you create <u>George</u> and he creates you; which is what we mean by "co-creation." We'll have another look at this phenomenon in Chapter 12. It may have more reality for you then.

What we would love to have you get is the following cognition on as many different levels as possible: *No one, appearances to the contrary, changes anyone else.* (For example, "I didn't know what to do until I talked with my psychiatrist . . . my minister . . . my parole officer . . . but once I did talk with him, he straightened me out." No, *he* didn't. He merely presented you with a picture of what you might possibly do, and you then agreed to do it. All relationships work by agreements—perhaps we should have said this earlier. "I" cannot change "your" behavior. What I can do is make conditions so unpleasant for you that you agree to change your behavior in order to protect your physical survival. Period.) SO FORGET TRYING TO CHANGE SOMEBODY ELSE... EVEN IF IT'S FOR "THEIR OWN GOOD." IT SIMPLY DOESN'T WORK. But you *can* change *your own* opinions, considerations on, prejudices about, and behavior toward another or others! And once *you* change *you*, your relationships with everybody else will change, too, and for the better.

Our present level of technology has not yet explored very far the vast amount of telepathic communications which exist between us. Right now, we call these links "vibes." Vibes are the quintessence of what we mean when we talk about flows.

If I am angry at and contemptuous of you, I need not express this verbally in order for you to know it. My "vibes" will tell you. Now, no one can change my vibes except me, but when they do change, you will notice that I am no longer building a barricade of hostility between me and you, and our relationship will change. You will be much more willing to flow good will back at me if I am not being overtly or covertly mistrustful of and skeptical toward you. (Who knows? We might even start curling up together again, even though at first, we each tend to keep one eye open.)

- a) How could I trust you?
- b) How could you trust me?
- c) How could you trust yourself?
- d) How could I trust myself?
- e) How could you trust another?
- f) How could another trust you?
- g) How could another trust another?

... is the way this drill is run between you and Him or Her. It suddenly occurs to us that a common error could be made on these drills in which "Henrietta" and "George" (a couple, just like any other here in Normalville, save for the fact that they are having their troubles... bring up the organ music, please) are participating. Let us illustrate what this error is:

Absolutely Wrong (Incorrect) Way to Run a One-on-One Drill:

GEORGE (asks Henrietta): How could I trust you? (Henrietta replies; George acknowledges her.)

HENRIETTA (asks George): How could you trust me? (George answers; Henrietta acknowledges.)
GEORGE (asks Henrietta): How could you trust yourself? (She replies; he acknowledges.)
HENRIETTA (asks George): How could I trust myself? (etc., etc.)

Running a drill this way will add ten hours onto its time before either of you gets a lift from it.

These drills are out to untangle snarled up mental circuits, and the fastest and most efficient way to do this is to have a person assume every possible point of view on that ensnarled circuit. Rapidly approaching the fouled circuit from east, west, north, south, and points in between eventually untangles it. So if George sets out asking Henrietta these questions and acknowledging her answers, George remains the Asker until Henrietta has answered all seven questions. Only then do they trade places.

When you are working with your Special Other, it is just fine for you two to alternate sets, but only when one of you has completely finished a cycle. Is this clear?

Looking at the areas of betrayal and trust regularly and repetitively will eventually bring anyone, no matter how embittered, to the space where he can read and appreciate wholly that hymn to sanity that Fritz Perls called "A Gestalt Prayer." It has been widely reproduced and, at least a couple of years ago, was a staple of every "headshop" in the country. Two people walking through a natural locale of great beauty and, superimposed somewhere on the landscape, the words: "You do your thing and I'll do mine, etc."

Most winning relationships work on the guidelines set forth in this "Prayer."

Enforce

Get a definition of what "to enforce" means to you (". . . been elected sheriff of this county and it's mah solemn duty to uphold the law and to enforce it. What's the brand name on that there cigarette, boy?"). Once you and your emotionally uninvolved friend have arrived at a definition of "enforce" that is real to you

Sharing Flows

and once your friend has arrived at a definition of this term that is real to him, he will ask you these questions:

a) What standard could you enforce on _____?
b) What standard could _____ enforce on you?
c) What standard could you enforce upon yourself?
d) What standard could _____ enforce upon himself or herself?
e) What standard could _____ enforce upon another?
f) What standard could another enforce on _____?
g) What standard could another enforce upon another?

The purpose of the drill is self-evident. It is obviously out after those standards which still stand between the open and free flow from you to _____.

If you run this drill with your Special Other, we suggest the following format:

a) In this relationship, what standard have I enforced on you?
b) In this relationship, what standard have you enforced on me?
c) In this relationship, what standard have you enforced upon yourself?
d) In this relationship, what standard have I enforced upon myself?
e) In this relationship, what standard have you enforced upon another?
f) In this relationship, what standard has another enforced on you?
g) In this relationship, what standard has another enforced on another?

(The last question on this drill can clear up a lot of what has been called "in-law trouble.")

Please

"Try as I may, I just can't ever seem to please that man...."

"I don't know what the hell she wants. Nothing I ever do is good enough for her!"

Have you never heard someone voicing either of the above two pitiful plaints? If you haven't, what cave in which Himalaya have you been meditating in the past dozen years? Because one of the major areas in which trouble breaks out between two terminals is in one believing that he is unable to please the other. Every year, some M.D. or another makes a fortune writing a book on the theme of: How to Please Her (Him) In Bed so that He'll (She'll) Love You Always and Never Leave You for That Tennis Pro (or Sexy Redheaded Secretary). Mostly what books like this expound are physical techniques of dispensing pleasure, and they will make you a first-rate if rather mechanical courtesan or gigolo, but in the main the entire area of "please" is not broached.

Another very common trap that many of us fall into is that of confusing *pleasing* with *propitiating.* "Okay, okay, okay, you can open that charge account at Bonwit's" (I'll do anything to get you to quit harping at me) or "Of course, I'll go to that (yuk!) X-rated movie with you, George. . . ." (I'm so beaten down by your accusations of being an example of Victorian morality that I'll do anything).

"Anything you say, dear."

Before casting off your mooring lines into the deep waters of this drill, define the verb "please." Then answer the following questions over and over again until you start to see that the verbs *please, help, co-create,* and *share* all mean just about the same thing.

a) How could you please _____?
b) How could _____ please you?
c) How could you please yourself?
d) How could _____ please himself or herself?
e) How could _____ please another?
f) How could another please _____?
g) How could another please another?

Another benefit from running this drill is that it brings you to a space where you realize that you know "George" or "Henrietta" a great deal better than you may have thought you did. And that, aside from the fact that he's always resisting taking an active interest in the garden club and you couldn't care less whether the Knicks get into the play-offs or not, he's still a pretty good old boy. And, also, that you got into your relationship with

Sharing Flows　　　　　　　　　　　　　　　　　　　　　　　　**109**

him out of your own free will (with maybe only a slight assist from Mother Nature).

Run with your Special Other, this drill can also dredge up areas of withheld desires which you have very politely left unvoiced for fear of "hurting her feelings" or "putting too much pressure on him."

 a) How could I please you?
 b) How could you please me?
 c) How could you please yourself?
 d) How could I please myself?
 e) How could you please another?
 f) How could another please you?
 g) How could another please another?

Continue running this drill until you see Her as she is, and that as-she-is is fine with you, or until you see Him as he is, and that as-he-is is a-okay with you. (Whether or not you then decide to go out and have an affair with her best friend or take a vacation to Acapulco with that jet-set Italian prince is a matter of preference on your part. *He* will not have failed to please you or *she* won't have not pleased you, it's just that you would prefer to share some time with somebody else. But it won't be all *His*, or all *Her*, fault that you went out and did what you were intending to do all along anyway.)

Responsibility

Which brings us to the not inconsequential area of RESPONSIBILITY that, in an age which prizes freedom above just about all else, is a very central issue to all relationships.

We cannot repeat our contention often enough: *A person does his own changing*. All you can do is to help him shift his attention around by making new options available to him or by showing him that what he had been considering an impasse is merely a tool whose use he has not yet discerned. But it is *he* who shifts *his* attention to the new option and it is *he* who takes *his* attention off his supposed limitations.

A person is thus responsible for making (or for not making) his own changes as regards outlook, preference, area of action, and life-style. If you have ever despaired of another—

"Dad'll never change. He just won't relax. He'll work himself to death!"

or, "I can't do a thing with that kid of mine!"

or, "George just won't stop playing the horses (or drinking or shooting dope . . . whatever),"

then please stop, right now. You are responsible for your life and its living—I am not responsible for yours (nor are you for mine), and if I start believing that I am responsible for improving you, then I am truly an egotistical moron and I deserve the heartbreak you will almost invariably present me with (only it'll be my heartbreak, but I'll be blaming you for it).

So, start out by defining responsibility. Then have your friend ask you the following questions. In the blank spaces provided, he places the name (which you have given him in advance) of the person whose behavior is upsetting the serene surface and the swirling depths of your life. If there are more than one of these people whose behavior is bothering you, "taking years off your life and giving you an ulcer," make a list.

a) How could you change _____?
b) How could _____ change you?
c) How could you change yourself?
d) How could _____ change himself or herself?
e) How could _____ change another?
f) How could another change _____?
g) How could another change another?

Run this drill until you see that _____ is a free agent who is just doing, in Fritz Perls' line, his or her "own thing." And that _____ will decide to change exactly when _____ decides to change, and not one moment before. And if _____ is caught up in a destructive game, then it is a self-destructive game which, presumably, _____ enjoys playing, no matter what other story _____ hands you or anyone else he or she can get to listen.

If you are running this drill with your Special Other, here's how it goes:

a) How could I change you?
b) How could you change me?

    c) How could you change yourself?
    d) How could I change myself?
    e) How could you change another?
    f) How could another change you?
    g) How could another change another?

Each of you takes turns running this until each of you comes truly to appreciate the immortal words of that wisest of all pre-Socratic philosophers, Anonymous, who once remarked: "You can lead a horse to water, but you can't make him drink."

Responsibility Continued

"Just look what you made me do—it's all your fault!"

"I vas chust obeyink orderz. I know nossing of zese atrocities. I vas only a pastry cook at Treblinka."

"But you *told* me to do it!"

He who buys these stories is the Number One Dumb-dumb. THERE ARE *NO* OFFERS YOU CAN'T REFUSE. THERE ARE *NO* SUGGESTIONS YOU HAVE TO FOLLOW. THERE ARE *NO* ORDERS YOU CAN'T DISOBEY.

Okay, sure, I may have told you to walk into that wall, but who did the walking?

And I may have told you to give me your life savings to invest in square wheels, but who gave me the money?

And I may have ordered you to shoot every Asian on sight while you and your platoon were out consolidating our gains in Vietnam, but who pulled the trigger?

Run the following drill until you really get the fact that, when push comes to shove, you are *free*.

Take the name of the person whose behavior most troubles you, and have a friend ask you the following questions:

    a) How could you be responsible for _____?
    b) How could _____ be responsible for you?
    c) How could you be responsible for yourself?
    d) How could _____ be responsible for himself?
    e) How could _____ be responsible for another?
    f) How could another be responsible for _____?
    g) How could another be responsible for another?

If you are asking these questions of your friend and he says: "Well, the domestic relations court judge told me I had to pay Henrietta x-number of dollars a month alimony," acknowledge his answer thusly: "Thank you for telling me what the court said. I will repeat the question: How could *you* be responsible for Henrietta?" And stay with this question until your friend runs out of evasive maneuvers and answers it.

Here is the one-on-one version that you and your Special Other can take turns running on each other:

a) How could I be responsible for you?
b) How could you be responsible for me?
c) How could you be responsible for yourself?
d) How could I be responsible for myself?
e) How could you be responsible for another?
f) How could another be responsible for you?
g) How could another be responsible for another?

This is an open-ended drill; you can run it—literally—forever. Instead, take it to a place where you truly get the fact that if you are walking down the street and a grand piano falls on top of you, you are responsible for being at the wrong place in the wrong time.

In the course of running this drill, the following cliches will probably come up for your inspection: The Jewish mother cliche; "I worry about you constantly, so how come you don't write?" (Who is it who's creating the worrying? And who is it who doesn't have anything better to do than to worry? Hmmm?) The concerned, nondenominational parent cliche: "Here's your new toy. Be sure to take good care of it, and don't break it!" (Whose toy is it really?) There is the equal opportunity cliche for all blackmailing spouses (white-mailing/beige-mailing) "You're making me sick with your behavior." (Oh, really? Who is making whom sick? Look at it.)

All these cliches are part of the big lie we tell about responsibility. Invariably, we tell the lie to ourselves, as in the case of: "Boy, I got drunker than a skunk last night at the party—sure hope I didn't make an ass out of myself!" Now, this citizen was having fun and he enjoyed getting drunk—terrific, good for him. But, in the next breath, he invalidates his own creativity by buying society's stories on what "good behavior" is. He is acting nonresponsibly.

Irresponsible behavior is freedom—"I do my thing."

Responsible behavior is freedom—"I am willing to be at cause over my behavior and I am willing to have it exactly the way it is."

Nonresponsible behavior wherein "I" go through life accepting other's determinations of what is good and what is bad leads to a very thwarted life. Ultimately, this type of behavior not only stultifies a person but also every other whom he can tyrannize (or, in actuality, who allows himself to be tyrannized). To repeat:

I cannot make you sick.
I cannot make you worry.
You can only make me feel guilty if I let you.
And . . . if it's my toy, how come I can't do what I want with it?

Anything you are willing to be at cause over and responsible for, you can have and can do something about. *Anything* you are unwilling to be at cause over will have you. ("See, my father used to beat me up when I was a kid, and that's how come I'm such a nebbish in my present life. It's all his fault, see. I never got enough love, poor pitiful me. . . .") This law applies to every area of human endeavor. For example: "I've got this swelling under my left breast, but I'm too afraid to go to the doctor for a checkup to see whether or not it's malignant, and here I am next year pushing up daisies". Or: "I've got this problem with George, he won't stop chasing younger women, but I'll pretend it doesn't exist 'cause there are some boats you just don't rock and, what was that? You say he cleaned out our joint bank account and has gone off to Brazil. . . ?"

All these are examples of nonresponsible behavior. We mention them not to throw stones at anyone, but because they need mentioning. It is currently fashionable to make excuses for ourselves and for the behavior of others. Making excuses will never result in a person's getting free—and it is also currently fashionable to aspire towards ever-increasing freedom. (One of the reasons our times are so confused and so turbulent is because the idea of excusing any and everything is banging head-on into the idea of freedom. And we all know how powerful an idea is whose time has come about.)

America's foremost literary critic, the late Edmund Wilson, knew a great deal about aesthetics and had a keen sensitivity to moral niceties and nuances. However, for the life of him, he could never figure out why, year after year, the vast majority of the public read (to the extent that they read at all) detective thrillers. And, more recently, Arthur Janov, Ph.D., a spokesman for sane and "straight" behavior, was interviewed on a nationwide TV network. The question posed this clinical psychologist was: Why are disaster films (like *Earthquake; The Poseidon Adventure; Towering Inferno, et al.*) so popular in the mid-1970s? He, like Edmund Wilson of the generation before him, was at a loss for an answer as to why we-the-people are fascinated by "escapist fare."

A reason why we avidly gobble up mysteries and pay out three bucks a head to see disasters might possibly be because we enjoy reading about heroes or seeing actors *take responsibility* for a lousy situation and, responsibility taken, going out and doing something about it. In "real" life, where the script is not already written, edited, and approved beforehand, lousy situations occur quite often. A person who finds himself in a jam wants no part of that jam. By his resisting having it, it becomes a lousy situation. If that same person were willing to confront it and to have it, that "jam" or "lousy situation" would become transformed into an interesting situation which his causativeness over would then give him the option of either handling or experiencing in and of itself; of either becoming at cause over it or of being its effect.

The difference between the standard-model stick-shift jerk citizen and the hero is that a hero is willing to have a situation as it is and then to change it—or attempt to change it—in a way that is pleasing and profitable to him, while the standard-model citizen does nothing except perhaps complain.

The moral of this chapter, if not this entire book, is simply that *if you are willing to be at cause over whatever happens to and around you, the quality of your life will improve instantly and the change will endure for just as long as you are willing to assume responsibility over your actions, your reactions, and your co-created actions.*

Get to a space where if I punch you in the nose you are willing to be at cause over the punch, and you can proceed enthusiastically in any number of ways. You can forgive me; you can karate chop me; you can turn tail and run; you can do anything you want to and stay in command of the situation as long as you don't fall into the trap of blaming me (and, by extension, an indifferent fate that could have allowed such a rank act of violence to happen). As soon as you start blaming me, or the stars, of the fact that my parents didn't love me enough when I was a kid and *that's* why I'm so hostile, I've got you . . . (sucker).

But if you take *responsibility* for my punch, then you can walk off and leave me—"This nut may be a psychopath; I better split before he draws a gun. Shame on me for not having spotted his symptoms before getting anywhere near him"—and the situation which I have provoked will not overwhelm you. You will not in turn put yourself through all kinds of agonies reliving the situation, wondering if you behaved in a manner commensurate with your standard of manhood, etc. You will not have your flow of attention hung up on trivia but will be able to sally forth and project your attention on those areas that truly interest you.

Because

In other words, you will lead a life devoid of *becauses*. And if you can rid your life of *becauses*, not only will the quality of your life improve, but your relationships will flourish. You will get to a place where you truly know that *no one is at willing cause over your life and relationships except you.*

> He hit me.
> I took his best punch.
> And I walked away.
> Period. End of the matter.
> *or:* He hit me.

I took his punch.
And I flattened him.
The End.

Becauses are one of the great traps we fall into. "I love you" vs. "I love you because you've got blue eyes and so does Doris Day and so does my Aunt Lil, and I love her . . . so how come you can't sing like Doris and you're not sweet like Aunt Lil?"

"He hit me because he's black and I'm white and he's got a justifiable grievance because of the way my race has treated his race down through history and, damn it, why does my nose keep on throbbing? He didn't hit me that hard and it was a week ago that he punched me. . . ."

Any time you tack a *because* onto an event, that event is able to exert a tremendously disproportionate amount of influence on your life and it will hamper and curtail your living. *Becauses* hang up your attention.

There is no limit to the number of *becauses* which can be pulled in on an occurrence in space and time. "They wouldn't hire me at IBM because I've only got a third-grade education. Boohoo . . . sob . . . moan . . ."

Some of the most intelligent people I know spend enormous amounts of their life justifying their dreams, their thoughts, their desires, and their actions. By my standards (which I am free to have or not have), they're wasting a lot of their time, but as long as they're happy doing it, I wish them an endless supply of justifications.

Run the responsibility drills we're presenting you with until you really see that *becauses* don't count: They are out-of-present-time creations tacked onto what is actually taking place in order to confuse the issue and to impede your taking responsibility for having it.

a) How could you help a because-maker?
b) How could a because-maker help you?
c) How could you help yourself?
d) How could a because-maker help himself or herself?
e) How could a because-maker help another?
f) How could another help a because-maker?

g) How could a because-maker help a because-maker?
h) How could another help another?

This is a rather awkward drill to run, but if you get into it, you will in a relatively short period of time arrive at a causative space over your rationalizations and justifications. When they are spotted, confronted, and handled, literally new horizons toward which you can project your own creativity will reveal themselves. It will be farewell, so long, and goodbye to:

> Oh, I couldn't ever take up painting because I can't paint a masterpiece right off the bat, even though I've always wanted to paint . . .
> *or:* I can't pursue my interest in the tuba because Henrietta won't let me practice . . .
> *or:* I never get to play bridge because George won't let me play cards . . .

and it will also be goodbye to such subtle traps as:

> She does everything I tell her. She's so helpless, poor dear, she can't even go to the supermarket unless I make out a shopping list for her in advance. Damn tootin', I'm responsible for her!

Goodbye to the entire bullshit world and hello newfound freedom.

Help Revisited

Now that you have examined your role in the creating of a certain number of areas (aberrant ideas which will tend to sabotage your relations with other individuals), it seems like a good idea to have you take another look at the concept of "help." By now, you will probably begin to see just how basic a flow help is, and also that it is virtually impossible *not* to help another. This is a huge insight, and is at the core of the entire Aquarian Age, whose birth pangs many people believe we-as-a-culture are collectively experiencing. When enough of us truly get that, as the *I Ching* has been saying for the past several millenia, there is *no blame,* and hence no overwhelming need to embark upon punitive measures or to seek revenge, this new age may indeed have been said to have reached the toddler stage.

Many people already have attained a psychospiritual plateau in which they do not blame others for whatever befalls them which they do not enjoy. . . . "Yeah, okay, so she left me, but I learned a lot from her. And while we were together we shared some really fine times."

Run the following sets of questions either with your well-intentioned-but-uninvolved friend* or with your Special Other until you get that, appearances to the contrary, *it's impossible not to help another in a relationship.*

How could you not help _____?
How could _____ not help you?
How could you not help yourself?
How could _____ not help himself or herself?
How could _____ not help another?
How could another not help _____?
How could another not help another?

How could I not help you?
How could you not help me?
How could you not help yourself?
How could I not help myself?
How could you not help another?
How could another not help you?
How could another not help another?

After you have run either version of these drills for sufficient time for you to get the paradox that my not helping you in our relationship is a consideration that you create and a deviation from what really happens, go back and run the questions regarding "help" again—if you feel like it.

How could you help _____?
How could _____ help you? etc.
or
How could I help you?
How could you help me? etc.

---
*Incidentally, your friend who patiently asks and acknowledges these questions will be surprised by deriving approximately as much benefit out of looking at these areas of flawed flows as you yourself do by directly examining your creativity regarding them.

Run these until you truly see and get that the instant I agree to share time/energy/space/matter with you, I am helping you. And vice versa.

Before sending you on to progressively heavier drills, it's probably wise for you to examine two additional areas in which flows become blocked, and when they do, suffering occurs.

Need and Love

As far as need goes, there are three cans of worms that are usually very entangled whenever this subject becomes broached. There is that of the hidden (subliminal) standard that must be met:

> I really needed my mother, but she was never there for me when I was a kid. So now I go through woman after woman symbolically searching for her. Eureka! I've met Henrietta who has the disposition of an irritated Doberman pinscher, and I'm in love! She makes me behave . . .

And very close to this lies the area of the Perpetual Garden of Peter Pan, which works as follows: *I resolve* (subliminally) *never to grow up* and which is most visible in the following examples:

I can't cook—you cook for me. (I need you . . .)
I can't make a living. You support me. (I really need you . . .)
I can't get any other girl in town to go to bed with me (I really, really, really need you, baby!)

Needs are only tough to become causative over because *we have never bothered to notice that we are not infants anymore.* Now, there's nothing wrong with being an infant when you're 35, except that you go around feeling so goddamn helpless all the time and getting laughed at by your contemporaries. I know whereof I speak. I was once in a very high-priced therapy whose tenet was that if only each of us would regress and feel to the fullest all our supposedly unmet infantile needs, our "neuroses" would be cured. I bought this story, and for three long years, worked hard to regress back to my pablum and diaper days. Needless to say, I was a total pain-in-the-ass to be around and I experienced a great deal of difficulty attempting to play the role of someone's employee/someone's father/and Uncle Sam's taxpayer. All I did was dramatize my needs for a warm mommy and a kind daddy until even I was bored. However, need is a very seductive trap to fall into, and I might still be back on the floor of a dark room wailing like a wet-diapered one-year-old if my co-author hadn't taken me aside and invited me to take a look at Need from every possible point of view.

Having made this confession, I now invite you to have a look at your own needs. As always in this chapter, the "need drill" begins with the version wherein you are working with a friendly but not overly concerned other, *i.e.*, somebody who likes you a lot but who doesn't take your problems all that seriously. (Someone who can ask you, "Hey, are you bragging or complaining?" and still remain your friend.) Divulge to him the name of your Special Other, and your friend then asks you the following questions about your Special Other:

    a) How could you need _____?
    b) How could _____ need you?
    c) How could you need yourself?
    d) How could _____ need himself or herself?
    e) How could _____ need another?
    f) How could another need _____?
    g) How could another need another?

How could I need thee? Come, let me count the ways! Being *wanted* is a beautiful validation of one's being. Being *needed* is a drain on one's ability to be. These drills will handle this particular area, too, because after you start running them for awhile you'll come to see that validating another's needs will drive him or her right down into a state of chronic incapacity to function and you'll be down there in diaper-land along with that needy person, too. *There is no one over twelve who can't survive on his or her own.* If two people come together in a mutually created relationship, they do so because having the relationship is more fun than being alone. To make this computation rationally is to go far towards ensuring the fact that you and the other person will indeed have a winning relationship, *i.e.*, one in which you win and so does the other. It is very, very, very hard to have a winning relationship with someone who needs you or who needs the relationship.

Another area that this drill uncovers is the difference between needs and preferences. For instance, you do not need a color TV, a house with a pool, a brand-new car, credit cards, country clubs, and beer-flavored ice cream, but many of us get ourselves into the bind of believing that we do need these luxuries to exist. Thus, when it seems as though the luxuries can no longer be acquired (for one reason or another), many such people make the computation that Life Is No Longer Worth Living. Take a look at your needs long enough and you'll be able to choose those which you prefer to have and those which you prefer not to have. (And if you get to this space, and you still pay attention to the world's inexhaustible supply of Jeremiahs—but smoking is bad for you; alcohol's a poison; beefsteaks wreak havoc on your digestive enzymes; swimming pools are a sign of decadence, etc., then shame on you for buying somebody else's ready-made story.)

a) How could I need you?
b) How could you need me?
c) How could you need yourself?
d) How could I need myself?
e) How could you need another?
f) How could another need you?
g) How could another need another?

is the way that you and your "George" or "Henrietta" run this drill when you're working together.

Love

Loving with no expectations, standards, or limitations puts a human into approximately the same space as a god. This type of love is so far removed from the state of being in love as to be virtually, but not wholly, a different state.

Loving is a state that is really quite native to us—being in love is thrilling, but it is such a trap as to be practically an aberration. Ovid was the first person we know of in the West* to call our attention to the "madness" that accompanies the state of being in love, but since his time a gradual groundswell of rejecting the in-love state has been slowly building. In the last ten years it has become something of a *tsunami*. Even kids know by now that, unless they worked very hard at it, Juliet would outgrow her relationship with Romeo or Romeo would meet Bianca and feel that same sharp, sweet bolt of lightning etching its way into his groaning groin and heart.

In fact, if the state of "I'm in love with you" lasted, the great bulk of this book would not be concerned with the male-female thing and, if there were even a need for it, it would be a pamphlet.

Define "love." Once you have done so and have arrived at a fairly stable definition (remember, every definition we ask you to create in this book serves merely as a mental jumping-off place and is entirely subject to revision), have your partner run you through the following drill many times over:

a) How could you love Henrietta?
b) How could Henrietta love you?
c) How could you love yourself?
d) How could Henrietta love herself?
e) How could Henrietta love another?
f) How could another love Henrietta?
g) How could another love another?

"L'amour, c'est ce qui se passe entre deux personnes qui s'aiment," said the French actor/artist/man of the world, Sacha Guitry. "Love is what happens between two people who love each other." Very, very true, this. Love is also the willingness to share and to co-create and to have sharing and to have co-creation of similar segments of matter, energy, space, and time. We offer these two truisms as our definitions of love. They are so broad that you will be able to give them to your Special Other before running the following drill, and they are so bland as to

---

*Of course, the Lord Buddha perceived the question with extreme clarity but in a much larger context seven or eight hundred years before the birth of Ovid when he told us that desire equals suffering and that the path to free ourselves from endless suffering is to become unattached to everything and to everyone.

ruffle no one's feelings. However, if these definitions do not bite for you, invent ones that are more perfectly tailored to your own tastes. Then run this drill:
- a) How could I love you?
- b) How could you love me?
- c) How could you love yourself?
- d) How could I love myself?
- e) How could you love another?
- f) How could another love you?
- g) How could another love another?

The last drill in this chapter is concerned with bringing you to see for yourself that, try as we may, we have to work extremely hard not to love one another. We have to apply ourselves to creating great amounts of space and time and matter and energy standing between us and keeping us at cross-purposes. However, we are truly a brilliant, creative species, and we have learned how to do this—and at what cost!—like maestros.
- a) How could you fail to love _____?
- b) How could _____ fail to love you?
- c) How could you fail to love yourself?
- d) How could _____ fail to love himself or herself?
- e) How could _____ fail to love another?
- f) How could another fail to love another?

Working with your Special Other, the drill, as you might imagine, goes thusly:
- a) How could I fail to love you?
- b) How could you fail to love me?
- c) How could you fail to love yourself?
- d) How could I fail to love myself?
- e) How could you fail to love another?
- f) How could another fail to love you?
- g) How could another fail to love another?

This has been a very preachy chapter, and so, before ending it, let us preach some more. The drills in this chapter are concerned with bringing you to a space where your flow of creativity towards another (or that whole collection of anothers called the world) becomes unblocked. What these drills, above all else, get you to do is to see in which areas of your creativity you have blocked flows. So even if you do not take an active part in any of these drills, the mere reading through the seven-part questions is going to give you a bit of a lift. Questions demand answers, and this being so, your merely having read them all will have meant that, subliminally, you will have answered them, too. But to get the greatest gain from these questions, you must bring your full attention to them. Now, this does, we admit, take time and effort. But since your relationships with the world are—unless you are a very enlightened person—just about all you've got, the time and effort you spend looking at all of these potential problem areas will be rewarded by your vastly increased ability and willingness to have relationships with people whom you at least initially liked. Chances are that once you've seen them, your affinity for them and flow of liking toward them will themselves have increased. True, we are not our brothers' keepers, but we are one another's brothers and sisters . . . and we are also friends, lovers, and partners, too. And it really is more fun to co-create having a relationship than to create not having one . . . or several . . . or many, isn't it?

9

A Short Chapter on Relationships Themselves

By your patiently and methodically working through the drills in the last chapter, you and _____ ought by now to have a good, open, free, and fresh flow going back and forth. However, the spectre of *the relationship itself* remains to be confronted.

This problem might be best encapsulated by the following, fairly often heard complaint: "Henrietta, I really like you, it's this goddamn state of being married I can't stand!" Or the obverse side of the same coin: "George, you're a really nice person; a fine, decent, considerable, sensitive man, but you haven't worked for eight months, and you haven't even tried to find a job in the last six, and I've had it supporting you!" In both of these cases, the other is okay; you can take or leave him and appreciate or deprecate his winning qualities, but it's the state of your relationship that galls and sorely tries you. Before junking the entire thing, please have a go at the following five drills.

Have a friend ask you the following seven questions, after you have both read and agreed with or disagreed with (and found something more appropriate) the following definition: *state of being overwhelmed*—that in which you are confronted with considerably more than you feel you can handle.

In the first blank space provided, your friend places the name of your particular relationship (*i.e.*, your marriage, your partnership, your family life, etc.); in the second blank space, your friend puts the name of that particular other with whom you are co-creating that relationship. He then asks you:

a) In relation to this (let us say "marriage"), how has (George) overwhelmed you?
b) In relation to this _____ , how have you overwhelmed _____ ?
c) In relation to this _____ , how have you overwhelmed yourself?
d) In relation to this _____ , how has _____ overwhelmed himself/herself?
e) In relation to this _____ , how has _____ overwhelmed another?
f) In relation to this _____ , how has another overwhelmed _____ ?
g) In relation to this _____ , how has another overwhelmed another?

Run with your particular other, this drill goes as follows:

a) In relation to our _____ , how have I overwhelmed you?
b) In relation to our _____ , how have you overwhelmed me?
c) In relation to our _____ , how have you overwhelmed yourself?
d) In relation to our _____ , how have I overwhelmed myself?
e) In relation to our _____ , how have you overwhelmed another?
f) In relation to our _____ , how has another overwhelmed you?
g) In relation to our _____ , how has another overwhelmed another?

By now, you ought to be up to running this particular drill with your special other and, in truth, both of you will probably get a lot of mileage out of that. Your relationship—the relationship itself—can't help but to improve.

Justifications

A justification is anything other than the event in question which we pull in to explain our behavior toward that event. It is the stuff of Ph.D. theses in the so-called humanities ("The Relationship of Charlotte Bronte's Wart to the Unfolding Aesthetic Patterns in *Jane Eyre*" in partial requirement of the Litt. degree) and it is also responsible for a great deal of experimenter bias in the harder sciences.

I, for example, am a grouch in the morning. This is the fact of the matter: Before 10:30 or so, speak to me at your peril. Now, if we are having a relationship and I bring to bear all kinds of rationalizations as to *why* I'm a grouch in the morning, what I am doing is (a) pulling in a whole bunch of causes to match an effect and (b) obscuring what is and (c) positing a whole bunch of extraneous creations that will stand between you and me. For outrageous instance:

> See, the reason I'm such a grouch in the morning is 'cause I had bad dreams and the reason I have them is cause I'm worried about you and the way that that guy we passed in the street yesterday looked at you, and I'm afraid you're cheating on me (but I'm more afraid of finding out that you are; and, aside from that, I'm even more afraid of our having a scene) so what I'll do is sublimate and compensate and have a dream whereby you're forcing me to protect you from this monster and I don't want to 'cause it'll eat me as well, and I wake up soaked in sweat and angry at you . . . and it's all your fault.

Or, if this is too "Freudian" for you (by and large, people go to analysts in order to learn how to perfect the subtle dialectical art of justification), take this example:

> *I leave the apartment and go for a walk.* (This is exactly what happened; the fact of the matter.) But the moment that I start pulling in *becauses* I also pull in all sorts of out-of-present-time creations which stand between me and the immediacy of my action. For instance:
>
> "I couldn't breathe in that apartment anymore!" (Because of this, I go for a walk.) "I want to get the chance to step on a lot of ant hills." (Because of this I go for a walk.)

"My Protestant work ethic won't permit me just to go for a walk, I must have a reason for going for a walk. So I went for a walk because I wanted to check out some property I'm thinking of buying... or I wanted to break in these new work boots... or my body needs exercise if it is to remain healthy and in perfect sync, therefore I went for a walk."

Do you see what we mean? There are infinitely more justifications to make than there are things to justify. I could create a million reasons why I had to take that walk. Not only would those million reasons tend to obscure the event-at-hand (a walk is a walk is a walk), but the creation of those reasons would tend to blow what is actually happening way out of proportion. Imagine, if you will, that I do something that you didn't like and you asked me *why* (oh, such a reasonable question!) and I started laying all kinds of stories on you. And you, litigious you, at each turn refused to accept my plausible explanation, thus forcing me to even wilder flights of fantasy and increasing amounts of irritation. Pretty soon, we would probably be in a full-fledged disagreement. "Tony, why are you such a grouch in the morning?"

"I'm a grouch in the morning because I'm a grouch in the morning. If you can just accept that, and accept me, and give me my space, we will get along okay." Good.

But if I start lashing back: "Well, why the hell do you always insist on my staying up to watch the Late Show with you? It was your idea to have the TV in the bedroom anyway! I can't ever get enough sleep blahblahblah..." and I wind up trying to justify my grouchiness by blaming it on you, we have got just cause for an argument and a withdrawal on both sides of affection. *And also* if I get sucked into your insidious little "why," then I am going to have to scour the physical universe for "Very Good Reasons Why" I'm a grouch, and the result will probably be the same.

So, even if you don't care to do either of the following two drills on justifications, do yourself a favor and forget the word *why* in your relationships. Whys really are loaded and, when asked in a naggingly insistent voice, they're like pulling a hair trigger:

She: Why didn't you clean the bathtub?
Why didn't you put out the cat?
Why didn't you dump the garbage?
He: Why did you run up that bill at Saks?
Why do you make so many toll calls?
Why isn't this coffee percolated?

to which
She replies: Why didn't you kiss me goodnight?
Why were you rude to my mother?
Why don't you like my kids?

(and God help him if he answers any of these questions). Let us assume he does not, but instead dredges up a few more *whys* of his own:

Why do you spend so much on groceries?
Why do you read *Playgirl?*
And why is *Playgirl's* centerfold cut out and hidden in the bottom drawer of your make-up table?
As a matter of fact, why do you spend so much time in front of a mirror?

... and so it goes. The seemingly innocent question *why,* coupled with enough justifications to fill a law library will, in time, lead to a lawyer's enrichment and your impoverishment, as well as to the annihilation of whatever form of relationship you formerly had.

Why'd you take that two-hour lunch Monday?
Why didn't you close that deal with Universal Vacuum?
Why do you smoke when we're discussing a new ad campaign with the people from the Heart Fund? As a matter of fact, why do you smoke?

Most of us will tolerate a certain amount of *whys* from our small children, but when our peers start asking this question, we construe *why* to mean *what's wrong with you,* and we react to this implied hostility with hostility of our own. (If you are in a relationship that you would really like to get out of, then deliberately start asking your co-relator *why* every time he says or does something, or whenever he fails to do something. If you will resolutely call him or her on everything at every turn, in a very short period of time he'll start hating you; a whole mountain of verbiage—a volcano of cant—will be standing between the two of you. Of course, physical violence might ensue, too, but if you survive it, it's a beautiful excuse for ending a relationship. "Boohoo! I can't stay married to a man who would even think of raising his hands to poor defenseless li'l old me! I want the station wagon, the stock options, the house, the bonds, and half your salary a month...." (Naturally, in this egalitarian age, it can work the other way, too: "I can't stay married to a woman who doesn't respect me and calls me a nitpicking, foul-tempered, impotent casuist! Why, that you can even entertain such thoughts shocks me so deeply that I'm going to file for divorce! I want the sports car, the stereo, the color TV, the stock options, the bonds, and the vibrator!")

If you wish to play this crummy part, the regular and frequent asking *why* will soon afford you ample opportunity to. If, however, you would like to improve your relationship with your Special Other, then sit down with him and write the following questions on a piece of paper:

a) In relation to our (marriage/partnership/association—whatever is appropriate), what have you justified?
b) How have you justified that? (The "that" refers to whatever the Responder says he has justified.)
c) How else have you justified that?
d) How else? ... How else? ... How else? Continue asking "how else?" until you have gotten all his undoubtedly numerous justifications. Once you have gotten them all, then ask him
e) What was it that was being justified?

After your Special Other answers this question, pass the card to him and he asks you these same questions.

Run this drill back and forth a few times. If there is still a pile of justifications standing between the two of you, have a go at the following drill:

a) In relation to our _____ , what has been justified?
b) In relation to our _____ , what has not been justified?

On Relationships Themselves

c) In relation to our _____, what is being justified?
d) In relation to our _____, what is not being justified?
e) In relation to our _____, what needs to be justified?
f) In relation to our _____, what does not need to be justified?

Now, a justification is almost the same as a rationalization, which in turn is almost the same as an explanation, which, itself, comes very near an excuse. Almost but not quite. This is a more important point than it may at first seem for this reason: Because a portion of our minds is so literal, we will tend to answer exactly the question that is asked us—i.e., if you ask me for a justification, I will give you what I consider to be a justification; I will not give you an excuse, a rationalization, or an explanation. And yet the lump sum of all of these tergiversations piles up between us. So in order to clean out the space we co-create in having a relationship, the following questions probably should be asked as well:

a) In relation to our _____, what has been rationalized?
b) In relation to our _____, what has not been rationalized?
c) In relation to our _____, what is being rationalized?
d) In relation to our _____, what is not being rationalized?
e) In relation to our _____, what needs to be rationalized?
f) In relation to our _____, what does not need to be rationalized?

a) In relation to our _____, what has been excused?*
b) In relation to our _____, what has not been excused?**
c) In relation to our _____, what is being excused?
d) In relation to our _____, what is not being excused?

---

*By writing all these questions in, we are not wasting space. We wish to furnish you with as few excuses as we possibly can not to run each of these apparently secondary drills. Questions on excuses can open up some very tangled cans of worms. For example, whenever anyone tells you that what you have done is inexcusable, you know that there is a serious impediment to your having a free, frank, and open relationship with that other.
**Both you and your Special Other ought to get a lot of mileage out of this question.

e) In relation to our _____ , what needs to be excused?
f) In relation to our _____ , what does not need to be excused?

And finally . . .
a) In relation to our _____ , what has been explained?
b) In relation to our _____ , what has not been explained?
c) In relation to our _____ , what is being explained?
d) In relation to our _____ , what is not being explained?
e) In relation to our _____ , what needs to be explained?
f) In relation to our _____ , what does not need to be explained?

As we have probably indicated, by now, you and your Special Other ought to be in a sufficiently good relationship that you can run these drills on each other directly. If, for any reason, you want to run them alone, you would run them exactly in the format given, only you would play both the Asker and the Responder's parts, and you would acknowledge each answer you made.

If you are running these drills with a friendly but detached other, give him or her the name of the person (or persons) with whom you are having relationship problems and put his name in all these drills where appropriate. (Also tell your friend the exact nature of your relationship with that person.) For example:

In relation to your <u>marriage</u> with <u>George</u>, what have you justified?
—Having mom come to live with us.
—Thank you. How have you justified that?
—Well, if it's true that two can live as cheaply as one, then three can live as cheaply as two. Hahaha.
—Thank you. How else have you justified that?
—By throwing a tantrum every time George scowls at mother.
—Thank you. How else?
—By threatening to leave him if he as much as dares suggest that mom go someplace else.
—Thank you. How else?
—By darning his socks, which I hate, just to keep him sweet.
—Thank you. How else?

On Relationships Themselves

—By appealing to his sense of mercy and justice: 'George', I always say, 'you wouldn't be heartless enough to turn a poor widow out into the cold, would you?'
—Got that. How else?
—By telling him if he makes a scene about mother, I'm insisting on a separate bedroom . . . across town.
—Okay. How else?
—By telling him what a heartless cur he is every time he complains when carrying out another case of empty gin bottles from mom's room. She only drinks for medicinal purposes, you know.
—Thank you. How else?
—That's all. There are no other justifications.
—All right. So what was it that was being justified?
—My mom's coming to live with us.

If this drill is being run with a friend who is not involved in your prime personal relationship, it acquires a second part. Your friend asks you:

In relation to your <u>marriage</u> with <u>George</u>, what has <u>George</u> justified?
—Coming home as seldom as possible.
—Thank you. How has <u>George</u> justified that?
—By actively disliking my mother and by always saying that we gang up against him.
—Okay. How else has <u>George</u> justified that?
—By saying that mother and I are female chauvinist pigs. I let him have it for that one.
—Got that. How else?
—By drinking up mom's medicine.
—Okay. How else?
—Oh, I don't know.
—Thank you. Invent a way.
—Oh, I guess by hanging out at The Magic Touch Massage Parlor a lot.
—Got that. How else? etc.

And when you have given him all of _____'s justifications, your friend then asks you: What was it that was being justified? (This last question tends to have you squarely confront the

134   RELATING

problem itself which, shorn of its many coats of justification, stands naked and exact and about which you can then form an exact opinion.)

If someone other than your Special Other is working with you, for all the other drills change the wording to fit the situation, *i.e.,*: "In relation to your <u>marriage</u>, what has been justified (or rationalized or excused or explained)? In relation to your _____ , what has not been justified (or rationalized or excused or explained)?" etc.

10

Competition, Phase One

As we stated at the beginning, traditionally our winning, as far as relationships are concerned, has been at our co-relator's expense. This is a habit that is deeply ingrained in many of us and, consequently, it demands a very thorough job of examining, because if you won't look and see what you are probably automatically doing, then you will continue to do it. And, as far as the Spirit of the Age goes, the so-called *Zeitgeist,* "my" winning at "your" expense, is slowly going out of fashion. More and more and more of us are seeing that this simply doesn't work any longer. Maybe we're starting to believe in the Indian concept of "karma," or, more probably, after two world wars, 25 years of cold war and the knowledge that another hot world war will kill off just about every sentient creature save the cockroach, the revolutionary proposition that *nobody wins if it's at someone else's expense* has finally acquired some respectability. The ecology movement has been an additional factor in this idea's coming of age. Moreover, there is a definite hunger in many of us for what *is*, not what *appears* to be, and a resulting impatience with false fronts and "images" as opposed to "gut-level truths." Our age-old standards aren't standing us in quite as good stead as they used to.

Philosophical pratings apart, here is how we are going to tackle the problem of competition which, even in the most loving relationships, will tend to surface after a while—especially in an era when women are redefining their roles in every conceivable manner. (As women acquire a broader latitude of action, men will naturally start to experience firsthand the slashing pangs of sexual jealousy which, in the main until now, has been a woman's special curse. But no longer. Now *all* of us are just about equally exposed to this most disruptive and degrading of feelings.)

The *very best* way to run the one drill we're presenting in this chapter is with a well-meaning but emotionally detached friend. Why? Because, inevitably, we crack back into standards here, and any time this area is broached, emotions ignite. As a matter of fact, we're only going to present a version that is to be run with a friend, but not with your Special Other. Safety first.

Part One

Tell your friend the name of your Special Other, your "Henrietta" or your "George."

Also, describe to your friend exactly what your relationship with that Special Other is, *i.e.*, "our marriage," "our partnership," "our one-night stand that's been running for twelve years. . . ."

Part Two

Have your friend ask you questions *a)* and *b)*, which are:
a) In relation to (Henrietta), what have you done or been or had, to make yourself right?

You answer this question. Your friend acknowledges the answer and writes it down. He then asks you the same question all over again:

In relation to _____ , what have you done or been or had, to make yourself right?

Again you answer this question. Again your answer is acknowledged and, again, it is written down on a list.

Your friend then asks you: *What else?* (By which he means; What else have you been or had or done, to make yourself right in your relation with good old _____ ?)

And he keeps on asking this question, "What else?" and you keep on answering it until you have covered everything you have done or been or had to make yourself right in relation to your particular Special Other. Your friend lists each response you make. Once your friend has all your answers and you have no further answers to give him, he then asks you;

b)   In your and _____'s relationship (name the relationship specifically, *i.e.*, "In yours and _____'s marriage..."), what have you done or been or had, to make yourself right?"

Answer this question. Your friend acknowledges your answer, and then he starts asking:

What else?
What else?
What else?
What else?
What else? What else? etc.;

and you answer him, and he writes each answer you make down in a list.

This is long and tedious to do, but in light of what comes next, it is most important.

Your friend then asks you:

Part Three

c)   In relation to _____ , what have you done or been or had to make another or others wrong?

You answer; he acknowledges then asks you:

What else?
What else?
What else? etc.,

and he writes down all your answers to these questions. When he has got them all, he asks you:

d)   In yours and _____'s (<u>marriage</u>), what have you been or done or had, to make another or others wrong?

You answer, your answer is acknowledged and written down, and your friend then starts asking you that long string of What Elses? You answer each "What Else?" and he writes it down.

e) He then asks you: In relation to _____ , what have you done or been or had, to keep yourself from being wrong?
>What else?
>What else?
>What else? etc.

You answer each of these questions, and he writes down each answer you make.

f) The next question he asks you is: In relation to yours and _____'s _____ , what have you been or done or had, to keep yourself from being wrong?
>What else?
>What else?
>etc.

Each time you answer, he writes down your answer.

g) The next question in this thorough drill is: In relation to _____ , what have you done or been or had, to keep another from being right?
>What else?
>What else?
>What else? etc.

h) In yours and _____'s _____ , what have you been or done or had to keep another from being right?
>What else, etc?

i) In your relationship with _____ , what have you done or been or had, in the interest of survival?
>What else, etc.?

j) In yours and _____'s _____ , what have you done or been or had, in the interest of survival?
>What else, etc.?

k) In your relationship with _____ , what have you done or been or had, to gain approval?
>What else, etc.?

l) In yours and _____'s _____ , what have you done or been or had, to gain approval?
>What else, etc.?

m) In your relationship with _____ , what have you done or been or had, to avoid disapproval?
>What else, etc.?

n) In yours and _____'s _____ , what have you been or done or had, to avoid disapproval?
>What else, etc.?

and finally; o) In your relationship with _____, what have you done or been or had, to acquire admiration?
What else, etc.?
p) In yours and _____'s _____, what have you done or been or had, to acquire admiration?*
What else, etc.?

Part Four

Together, you and your friend assess the list. Inevitably, the same items will crop up time and again—these are the ones you will not want to work with, but which should be worked with. Also, be particularly sensitive to outstandingly important items (such as a propensity on your part to pull in a lot of illness . . . "I'll make you care about me, if it kills me! If my sprained ankle won't work, then I'll contract malaria, and if that doesn't work, I'll get a heart condition . . .") and to oustandingly ridiculous items. The outstandingly ridiculous ones are just as vital in cleaning up your relationship with _____ as are the outstandingly important ones.

From a list of perhaps as few as five to as many as fifty items, you and your friend will arrive at three or four which you will then work with in Part Five.

Part Five

For the sake of illustration, let us assume that the first item on the pared-down list is something ridiculous like growing a beard.
Your friend then asks you the following questions:
1. In relation to "Henrietta," how has growing a beard made you right?"
Response; acknowledgment.

---

*Get answers to questions o) and p). Profound cognitions lie in this area—for instance: "Well, maybe I've thrown a tantrum and started a fight because, oh gosh, I mean it's really an awful thing to do, but the last fight we had, the neighbors came and they called the police who called the fire department, and Channel 7 Eyewitness News happened by, and . . . far be it from me ever to call attention to myself (I'm really the shy, retiring type), but Henrietta and I were in the papers (smirk) and we even were on television. Modesty compels me to admit that we had ourselves ONE HELL OF A BEAUTIFUL BRAWL. . . ." In other words, people will go very far to attract attention (which they construe as admiration). Who, for instance, had ever heard of Jack Ruby outside of Dallas before a November day in 1963? Or look at people who literally kill themselves to get their names in *The Guinness Book of Records*.

2. In yours and "Henrietta's" _____ , how has growing a beard made you right?

Response; acknowledgment.

Notice that questions 1 and 2 are very similar. But they are not quite exactly the same. The reason we are asking both sets of questions is to give you a double opportunity to answer questions you really don't want to. The questions in this long, tedious, and necessary drill deal with the prize skeletons in the most secret recesses of your closet; little gems of personal funkiness which, collectively, all make up the great subliminal computation: I SURVIVE BEST AT EVERYONE ELSE'S EXPENSE.

Sticking with the same ridiculous answer, "growing a beard," the next questions are:

3. In relation to _____ , how has growing a beard helped you win?

Response; acknowledgment.

4. In yours and _____'s _____ , how has growing a beard helped you win?

Response; acknowledgment.

5. In relation to _____ , how has growing a beard helped you avoid losing?

Response; acknowledgment.

6. In yours and _____'s _____ , how has growing a beard helped you avoid losing?

Response; acknowledgment.

7. In relation to _____ , what approval has growing a beard gotten you?

Response; acknowledgment.

8. In yours and _____'s _____ , what approval has growing a beard gotten you?

Response; acknowledgment.

9. In relation to _____ , what disapproval has growing a beard avoided?

Response; acknowledgment.

10. In yours and _____'s _____ , what disapproval has growing a beard avoided?

Response; acknowledgment.

11. In relation to _____ , how has growing a beard been admired?

Response; acknowledgment.

12. In yours and _____'s _____ , how has growing a beard been admired?
   Response; acknowledgment.

Have your friend run you through all twelve questions in Part Five of this drill on each item you have assessed as being either outstandingly important or outstandingly ridiculous. Realize that the answers you will make to these questions may and probably will go very, very far back in time. When you can spot their proper contexts (which, in most cases, will have very little to do with yours and _____'s relationship), a lot of your compulsive behavior toward _____ will disappear and, with it, a good deal of the tension that stands between _____ and you.

11

A Look at the Goal of Surviving: Competition, Phase Two

You've probably noticed how general the questions in our drills are and yet, paradoxically enough, what precise answers they elicit from you once you get into them. The reason for this is that, while each one of us has a vast array of uniquely personal experiences, the manner in which we become aberrant about our experience is pretty much the same. Aberrations are, by and large, a matter of goals and standards whose final unraveling is beyond the scope of this particular book.

However, since nearly all of us possess *survival* as a goal of overriding importance, having a winning relationship, or a whole slew of winning relationships, is going to be difficult as long as one particularly noxious aspect of the goal of survival remains unexamined, and this is: I SURVIVE BEST AT YOUR EXPENSE.

Now, few of us (Mafia dons excepted) are up to turning this assertion into a way of life. For one thing, it's no longer fashionable, and anyone who overtly adopts it as a code of conduct is going to find himself labeled a fascist or an imperialist or a slaver ... something unpleasant. And if you examine the failed relationships you have had with other people, you will perceive that just before the relationship terminated, one of you was accusing the other of doing just this . . . *you're exploiting me*, nyah, nyah, nyah. Why? How does this come about?

One of the ways it might is by our entering into a relationship with another because we feel that our survival is going to be improved through regular and frequent contact. If you ever made this computation on a less than totally conscious level (as I did) . . . if you ever got yourself into a relationship with another not for the fun of it, but because you felt your chances of survival would be greatly enhanced by doing so, then you embarked upon a life or death situation. And when your partner failed, for one reason or another, to match your unvoiced expectations—and how could he or she help but fail because you didn't even know you had them yourself?!—then all hell inevitably broke loose.

Since everyone's experiences in a desperately decaying relationship are different and yet the form the relationship assumes is pretty standard, we are going to generalize a bit. Forgive us. Thank you.

As a species, we are extremely insecure for we know that death awaits us. The problem is MY SURVIVAL. And it is likely that questions pertaining to my survival are going to enter into just about every plan I make, goal I postulate, path I pursue, and relationship I co-create.

So here I am, anxious about my survival. And here you are, anxious about yours. And I know I am going to die and you know you are, too, and so we're both—to a certain if unmeasured extent—*anxious*. But I meet you and what's more I enjoy you; when I'm with you, I really feel good. And you tell me you do as well.

Being delighted with you, I am no longer having to put my attention on the possibility of my not surviving at any given moment. I have you; I do not have to worry about eating peaches or whether or not my bald spot is showing. For the moment, Eros is triumphing over Thanatos.

But when you say or do something that reminds me of the fact that I not only have you, but I also have a whole mess of *anxiety* as well, I am going to start disliking you a little for this. I am depending on you to keep me surviving at my best, and the way I best survive is when my attention is not on my anxieties. (You 'n me against the world, babe . . . See, I can be open with you. I trust you. I feel reborn because of you. I'm a kid again. I don't have to worry when I'm with you . . . Whee! I'm "in" love and I'm safe *in* love. It's like a great big, co-created womb that I get to enjoy again. . . .)

But the more time and the more space that you and I share, the greater the probability that you are going to say or do something that reminds me about my anxieties, and the more you do this, the more ambivalently I am going to feel about you. Plus, you've got anxieties of your own—and I don't want any part of them; you don't either—but I start reminding you of them. After a while, my "in love" relationship with you is going to become one which the pyschs term "love-hate" wherein the following—always unspoken—assumptions come into play:

> I'm in love with you because you make me feel good, but you're reminding me of my anxieties now and so you don't make me feel good enough, and so I'm hating you a little bit, too.

From simultaneous flows of love and hate, *competition* is born.

How does this happen? Here I am, in love with you quite a lot and also in hate with you a little, and suddenly I'm competing with you and you're competing with me, and what's going on? Why are we competing? What are we competing for? (It's utter madness . . . or at least utter folly.)

Competition enters into the stark outlines of this unpleasant picture we're sketching because any anxiety having to do with survival *implies* (implies, mind you) the threat of loss—and loss cannot exist independently of winning.

But what, in a relationship, *is* there to win or lose? (Don't worry: Get yourself in the position of loving somebody else but also hating that somebody a little bit, and you will invent all kinds of ways of scoring points off that somebody else. Here is an eternally vast area of one-upspersonship. Here is an arena strewn with the bodies of a million slight cruelties. Here is where the uniquely personal heartaches of a failed relationship reside. This is, literally and symbolically, a ghost town. Here, too, is where one party starts accusing the other of exploitation.)

Now I never wanted to get here—I love you, goddammit!—I never wanted to find myself sniping away at (of all people!) you. Yet this is precisely what I'm doing. *Somehow or another,* I've gotten myself into a guerilla war with you. And I don't like it, and I want out, but I don't want to lose you!

What *is* competition?

What are its most basic and irreducible elements?

Surely, prior to all else, it's a matter of *flows.* Surely, in every competition there is a simultaneous and just about equal flow of attraction ("I love you, honey") and repulsion ("Give me my space! You're crowding me to death!"). And as long as these two flows are balanced, our relationship will continue to lurch along. Fits and starts. But as soon as the love aspect diminishes, as soon as the attraction aspect wanes, the hate or the repulsion aspect will wax and the tension inherent in the very ambiguity of the relationship will shatter the relationship into painfully sharp shards. This is what competition in a love relationship means.

Quite simply what it boils down to is this: *survival.* To survive is to win. I win more when I'm with you (so I'm in love with you) only now "you're" triggering my anxieties (which I want no part of) so I'm starting to lose. . . . This is how competition enters the relationship.

Since it is an unacknowledged competition it tends to persist automatically and the more "out of love with you" I get, the more it grows.

Finally, just before the bitter end, you and I are both competing *fiercely* for the right to survive itself! That this makes no rational sense whatever is beside the point—this is the way that souring relationships curdle. And this formula of applied madness cuts across the lines of all relationships—the son who must escape from the "domineering father" (which is by and large the WASP literary staple; think of Stephen Daedalus looking for his father; think of any of Thomas Wolfe's protagonists), or the son who must escape from the domineering mother (in the last twenty years, the Jewish literary staple) or, in this age of women's emergence as people, the wife who must escape from her husband. Survival appears to be what is at stake. And it really doesn't matter (except to you when you're in the situation) who your antagonist is, but notice that invariably your cry will be that of "You're Killing Me!"

This being the case, you'll notice that it is precisely in this area where the "juiciest murders" take place. Just last week, a Los Angeles paper reported that a woman deliberately ran over and dragged to death another lady whom her boyfriend had been seeing. And hardly a week goes by but what some husband shoots his wife. One might declare that it is the phenomenon of "sibling rivalry" translated to one's closest personal relator, "partner rivalry." Have you, for instance, ever looked at your mate in total incomprehending hatred and dismay as the thought flashed into your conscious awareness that 'I'm gonna get you before you get me?' Have you then ever wondered about the incredible intensity of murderous hatred that he or she appeared to inspire in you?

The fury, the dismay, the tremendous sense of overriding loss and utter futility which accompany this flash of a thought ('either you go or I do') is what we mean by *"partner rivalry."*

But *can* another honestly jeopardize my survival? Can You really bring Me to a point where I make the usually fatal computation that 'I'm gonna get you before you get me?' Or, 'I've gotta get you before you get me?' Let us see.

Let us take a long, hard look at survival itself in the following drill.

The drill is simplicity itself, but people who are locked into considering themselves the hapless effects of an incomprehensibly vast and numbingly indifferent universe will encounter difficulties running it. Its commands appear too paradoxical to be given credence. They are not.

However, the only way to resolve the seeming paradox that this drill apparently entails to your own satisfaction is for you to be willing to run the drill. And run it in the exact format in which we are going to present it. In this one version, you can run it alone (providing you're willing to acknowledge your answers) or with a friend of with your Special Other. The end phenomenon of this drill is "mystic" (or what consensus reality considers mystic) and was best expressed by Lao Tsu some three millenia ago: "Then, though you die/You shall not perish."*

Do the drill and stick with it until you know with absolute gut certainty that, appearances to the contrary, *there is no time you did not survive.* The you in question is not your body or that nexus of machinery you call your brain, and it is not this particular name and identity you are presently lugging around. It is, rather, the one element in your universe* that remains when all else is said and done and while all else is being done. Here is the drill:

a) Tell me a time you survived.
   Response; acknowledgment.
b) Tell me a time you thought you wouldn't survive.
   Response; acknowledgment.
c) Tell me a time you didn't survive.
   Response; acknowledgment.

Your willingness to look repetitively at this area of your experience is the key to this drill. Cycle through it as many times as you need to until you *know* that no matter what anybody the hell else did to you, you "somehow" survived. Truly to run this drill to a valid end-point is suddenly and irrevocably to lose a lot of the anxiety you're carrying around with you about body-death. And it is also to begin cracking into the first layers of the cosmic joke that so many enlightened masters have enjoyed at the world's (to say nothing of their former selves') expense.

This is a very heavy area insofar as emotional charge is concerned. Reactions to looking at this aspect of the goal of survival will vary: Some persons will bliss out; some will begin laughing or crying hysterically; others will be more indifferent—"Oh, that's nice. I'm immortal. I always rather suspected I was . . ."

---

*From "Poem No. 16" in *The Way of Life: Tao Te Ching,* translated by R.B. Blakney. New York. New American Library (Mentor Books), 1955.
*The term "universe" may seem a bizarre and inappropriate one to use here. If it puzzles and/or bothers you, take a look at our previous book, *Mind Games.*

When you have reached the point of intuitively knowing that you have survived everything from state funerals to lynchings to galaxies going nova, then give yourself (or have your partner give you) the following two commands:

- d) Cease creating these pictures. Tell me when you have.
Response; acknowledgment.
- e) Return to present-time. Tell me when you're right here, right now.
Response; acknowledgment.

One out of every, say, fifty or sixty people doing this drill is suddenly going to become horrified: "Oh no! You mean it doesn't end? There's no way out of this shit pile? It's going to go on forever!" To them, we offer these words of comfort: "Your universe will continue for as long as you continue to create it. If you are currently in the midst of a cycle of losses, cheer up; you have probably had trillions "before" and your losses will end as soon as you start creating winning cycles, of which you have probably had tens of trillions. Read *Mind Games* and do its drills."

One out of every 100 people is going to get stuck in a combination of horror and fascination as he or she watches a person intuitively known to be "me" dying in some particularly spectacular fashion. (Just as we tend to focus on the so-called "negative" qualities of people we meet, so we tend to focus on our most dramatic exits from this vale of tears. If you find yourself getting stuck in old scenes of murder, rape, ritual disembowelment, being buried alive, etc. (you always wondered where your claustrophobia came from, didn't you?), then forcibly bring yourself back to the here and now as follows. Have a friend turn to this page of the book and instruct you as follows:

> Walk that body of yours over to that wall right now . . . thank you. Take that body's right hand and have it touch that wall right now . . . thank you. You withdraw that right hand right now . . . thank you. Jump that body of yours up and down against this floor right now . . . thank you. Take that left hand of yours and have it touch the wall right now . . . thank you. Withdraw that left hand . . . thank you. Turn that body around right now and walk it

over to that table . . . thank you. With that body's right hand, touch that table top right now . . . thank you. Where is your nose right now? Show it to me . . . thank you. Touch that face's nose with your body's left hand right now . . . thank you. Come up to present-time, right now . . . thank you . . .

Continue doing this for as long as it takes to reorient the person in his or her body, which is a nice thing to have because it's always in present-time no matter how far afield your consciousness ranges.

Once the person has returned to present-time, ask him what it was he was looking at. Get details. Ask him:

1. When did the incident occur? Give me a date.
2. How long did the incident last?
3. What exactly happened?
4. Who was involved?
5. Was there an issue in question? Could it have involved standards?
6. What time of day or night did the incident take place?
7. What were your feelings during the incident?
8. Approximately how many times between the date of the incident and today have you been reminded of something similar?
9. Locate, very rapidly, and identify each and every one of those somewhat similar incidents and put them all in their proper order in space and time in relation to Right Now. Don't think about doing this, just do it!
10. Thank you. How does the incident seem to you right now?
    (And if it's still fascinating the person, have him tell it to you again and again until it loses its fascination. You might also remind the person that he does have a body which you see before you and, this being the case, whatever happened, gruesome as it was, couldn't have been all that devastating because here he is—surprise!—in another body.)

Most of you will not undergo anything as traumatic as this, however. You'll just look at a whole bunch of pictures that will be tantamount to seeing an old-time Hollywood "historical" movie. They will all be starring you, but you might experience some difficulty spotting yourself in all your manifestations. One in perhaps 1,000 will experience millions of pictures rushing by at incredible speed, something that happens apparently to many people when they ingest LSD or hashish oil. If you do, do not panic; you are merely taking a look at the way your mind works anyway and at all times from a perspective that is normally withheld from you by the inhibitory functions of your brain. Eventually the pictures will appear to cease (actually, you will merely readopt a more conventional point of view). However, if you feel that you've lost control of your mind, then start touching walls, tables, floors, objects—whose very object-ness is indisputably here/now—until your normal perceptions return.

So much for this drill, except to say that if you've ever been bothered about death, you will derive many and varied benefits from running it. Emotionally, psychologically, and spiritually you will feel a lot better for having been willing to look at this area of your supreme creativity.

Once you understand that all anyone else can do is *appear* to threaten your survival and can never really bring about your nonsurvival, you are ready to start looking at who controls your relationships. Who has power over them.

The next drill is better run with a friend or alone, unless your Special Other is keeping pace with your progress through this book and your consequent growth. Take a look at the items on the list below:

>affinity
>love
>understanding
>sharing
>safety
>comfort
>happiness
>physical pleasure
>joy
>suffering
>loneliness
>frustration
>tedium

Then determine which item comes closest to summing up your relationship with your Special Other. When you have identified it—and you may invent whatever term is appropriate: piles, hot flashes, mounds of debts, etc.—then tell your partner what the term is. Your partner then takes the term and, placing it in the blank spaces provided, asks you the following questions:

a) What is the source of _____ ?
   Response; acknowledgment.
b) Tell me about that.
c) What is not the source of _____ ?
   Response; acknowledgment.
d) Tell me about that.

A very profound insight stems from the repetitive running of this drill. It can assume two forms, either one of which is "correct." Heretofore, we've been feeding you the cognitive realizations that these drills produce. But now we won't. We're going to reserve the pleasure of discovery for you. Enjoy your heuristic delight.

Oh, one thing, though; if you are not totally certain what the word *source* means, consult your nearest dictionary.

The second part of this drill is exactly the same as the first only here, in the blank spaces provided, have your *partner* put the term that epitomizes your relationship with your Special Other. Take another look at our list to see if any of the terms we've provided apply. If not, feel free to invent the one that is most appropriate.

Once you have found it, reveal it to your partner and have him ask you the following questions on it.

a) What is the source of _____ ?
   Response; acknowledgment.
b) Tell me about that.
c) What is not the source of _____ ?
   Response; acknowledgment.
d) Tell me about that.

It may take you a while to cycle through one or both of these source drills, but do not begrudge the time spent. If you're not willing to look, then you won't, and if you don't look, you'll never see. The beauty of these repetitive questions is that each time you answer one of them you have to look.

A Brief Digression on Our Drills

Have you wondered by now why my coauthor and I ask you to run the drills in this book over and over and over and over?

The reason is that we all have so much buried in that great subliminal storehouse called (depending upon the thinker's affiliations) the Unconscious; the Collective Unconscious; the Subconscious; or the Reactive Bank. And repetition is a great method of making sure that you sort through enough material so that you finally begin to see exactly what *is* the problem at hand and how you can best solve it.

The questions (or commands) in the drills automatically summon up a certain number of answers or responses. They tend to come in clusters. The specific answer that will get you that much freer may be quite deeply buried beneath many layers of rationalizations, justifications, and a general unwillingness to have anything to do with the problem area the questions or commands delineate. So we have found that asking the same question over and over and over is rather like taking individual shovelfuls of dirt out of the ground you are excavating. Each shovelful appears to be the same, but the mire it brings up is each time a little different and the hole gets deeper. When enough of it gets cleared away, you then can see what lies buried under all the debris. Then, too, we must not forget the fact that

Let us assume that by now you have arrived at a profound insight into the way relationships work. A drill that intensifies and expands the startlingly beneficial range of the immediately preceding drill goes like this:

    a) What _____ are you free to originate?
    b) What _____ are you free to let _____ originate?
    c) What _____ are you free not to originate?
    d) What _____ is _____ free not to originate?

Explanation

    Let us take the drill line by line. The first item is: What _____ are you free to originate?

In the blank space provided, insert the term that best describes both what your Special Other *means* to you and what your relationship with him or her means to you. This will be whichever of the two terms you used in the drills about source, about which you feel the most strongly. Let us assume that, after much soul-searching, you have decided upon "joy." The first question would then read:

What <u>joy</u> are you free to originate?
The second question would read:
What <u>joy</u> are you free to let "<u>George</u>" or "<u>Henrietta</u>" originate?
The third question would be:
What <u>joy</u> are you free not to originate?
And the fourth question would be:
What <u>joy</u> is "George" or "Henrietta" free not to originate?

Continue cycling through this drill until you see on a deeper than intellectual level that, despite the staggering amount of fouled circuitry you have accumulated in your mind, you are a free agent in your relationship and so is your particular "George" or "Henrietta."

The final drill in this chapter reinforces the insights which its predecessors have afforded you. Have a friend ask you the following series of questions, repetitively:

a) In relation to (<u>the name of your Special Other</u>) , what is?
Response; acknowledgment.
b) In relation to _____ , what isn't?
Response; acknowledgment.

Don't worry about taking a long time to get through this drill. It is out to put you in touch (and, indeed, at cause over) a power you have probably not been exercising for quite some while.

12

For the Relationship That Just Won't Go

Exclusivity in relationships, especially love relationships, may come back into fashion in the next generation. Now, however, the pendulum of the times has swung the other way, and the stability that an exclusive relationship promises is no longer so highly prized. Everywhere the old, stabilizing influences have been swept aside by a frenzy of restless experimentation. In America, which has thus far been spared a radical socioeconomic upheaval, the restlessness of the times has gone into a search for self.

> Who am I really? What are my boundaries? What is this thing called self? How can I grow/how can the self grow?

It's almost as though a whole generation of Romantic rebels (a la Vigny, Poe, Byron, de Musset, Baudelaire, Rimbaud, etc.) has come of age since, say, 1960. Instead of rebellion for the sake of new forms of art, however, the emphasis seems to be on new dimensions of self. One of the strengths of such an attitudinal stance is its utter self-centeredness. . . . I focus on me. One of the weaknesses of such an attitudinal stance is that if all my attention is on me, I'm not going to be all that interested in you and, consequently, I'm not going to be willing to put a great deal of energy into building a relationship with you. The lonely seeker in his laboratory (the Simmelweisses, the Pasteurs of the 19th century) and the solitary genius of nineteenth century literature has been translated into the rap-session, consciousness-raising, *prahna* and astrology buff of the beginning of the Kennedy administration. LSD had a lot to do with showing us that there are new paths to pursue and different games to play, as of course did that other great pharmaceutical boon to our age, Enovid.

> Hey I'm into *me*!
> Doing my thing (baby).
> I'm takin' care of my business.
> Travelin' light and gettin' my shit together. . . .

These are the cries of the times. In such a climate of me-me-me, it is going to take a great deal of mutual willingness for a couple to stick together. Not that it's ever been easy, given those wonderful standards we all carry about inside our minds like so many Sisyphuses, but then, too, a predominately urban environment and a moderately high-level technology have combined to provide us with (a) a great variety of human bodies to relate to and (b) the promise of the ability—if only each of us stays young enough, strong enough, dedicated enough—to embrace our own particular, highly personal, custom-tailored life-style.

We have called this book *Relating* because we imagine that most people who read it will have already gone through a number of jobs and emotional partnerships and, to a certain extent, are engaged in living out Polonius's dictum: "This above all, to thine own self be true," which, if taken literally, is going to turn out some very opportunistic and cold-blooded pragmatists. Especially if no one is quite sure what that "self" is. So that Polonius's advice, 1970s version, might well read: If it feels good, do it.

In an age of revolutionary upheaval, the computation I SURVIVE BEST WHEN I TRAVEL LIGHT, ALONE, AND UNENCUMBERED becomes quite a force to reckon with. It is going to lead to a good many ruptured relationships because we have also learned that there is no viable way to force someone else to continue in a relationship with us if that someone else truly does not want to.

> Henrietta is just as powerful a creator as George is—and George knows it;
> Henrietta is just as aberrant as George—and Henrietta knows it;
> Henrietta is just as free as George is, and each of them is just as free as he or she is willing to be (this is the "message" of our book).

What all this mound of sociological cliche-gathering has to do with the purposes of our book is simply this: We get attached to people; the people for one reason or another (and there's always a good reason—how could you help a because-maker?) decide to sever the attachment (. . . no, please. I beg you. Not a sentimental, sloppy scene. This is hard on me, too. Let's have a clean break. I've learned so much from you. You'll always be my friend); and if we are the party that does not wish to sever the relationship, we're going to hurt like crazy. *Hurt like crazy.*

And we will continue hurting virtually indefinitely* until we get to a space where we start looking at the hurt and dissolving it. So if you are, or if you have ever been an occupant of Heartbreak Hotel, we strongly recommend your engaging in the following three drills. But they have the additional effect of bringing you to a place where you are at cause over your relationships, and hence might be profitably run by virtually anybody—male, female, or undecided.

Drill Number One goes as follows:

a) What conditions have been encountered with _____ ?
   Response; acknowledge.
b) What assumptions are involved?
   Response; acknowledgment.

---

*I don't know if anyone has ever done a clinical study on romantically rejected people, but I strongly suspect that it is possible to die of a "broken heart" or at least get very physically sick from one. Katherine Anne Porter wrote a famous short story, "The Jilting of Granny Weatherill." It is eminently worth reading if only to experience, secondhand, how long the pain of rejection can persist.

c) How's it been handled?
   Response; acknowledgment.
d) How is it right now?
   Response; acknowledgment.

Rather than go into a long, theoretical discussion extolling the virtues of this particular drill, we are going to present a taped transcript of a session in which my coauthor was the Asker and a young man, whom we will call "George" was the Responder. We will call George's lady "Henrietta."

LENNY: Okay. This is the session. Is there something I should know about you but don't before we get into it?

GEORGE: I'm angry. I'm jealous. I feel shitty. Henrietta's moved in with this guy she's been seeing. This is a dumb, adolescent way to feel but no shit, I want to die.

LENNY: Got that. So what conditions have been encountered with Henrietta?

GEORGE: A state of being in love with her.

LENNY: Thank you. What assumptions are involved?

GEORGE: Uh, assumptions . . . well, I guess that I'll always be in love with her. I've just always assumed that we were meant for each other.

LENNY: Thank you for telling me that. How is it right now?

GEORGE: I love her. I miss her. I can't stand the fact that she's left me.

LENNY: All righty. What conditions have been encountered with Henrietta?

GEORGE: She left me! I'm not good enough for her. I'm not man enough for her. People have been leaving me all my fucking life! I hate it!

LENNY: Thank you for telling me about what people have been doing to you. I will repeat the question: What conditions have you encountered with Henrietta?

GEORGE: Okay. She said she loved me; she said let's live together. So we did. Then she said, uh, I was too heavy for her; too serious, so she told me to get out. She'd call me every once in a while—whenever she felt like it—and we'd go out and, occasionally we'd be lovers. Then I didn't hear from her for a long time, and just after Christmas, she called and said that she'd been down in Mexico with him and that if I wanted the TV and the box spring back I'd better come get them because she'd moved out of her place. The last thing she said to me was that she'd left the key with her girlfriend.

So I rented a U-Haul, and a friend and I went to get my stuff and, when I got inside her apartment, I broke down and cried.

LENNY: Got that. What assumptions are involved?
GEORGE: That it's all over between us. The love of my life . . . it's turned into bullshit.
LENNY: Thank you. How's it been handled?
GEORGE: I wept! I'm still weeping inside. I'm sick of mourning her—I came to you, that's how I handled it.
LENNY: Okay. How is it right now?
GEORGE: A little better. *I* don't know. . . . If she called me on the phone right now and said, "Baby, come on over and see me," I'd be out the door just as scattered as buckshot.
LENNY: Got that. What conditions have been encountered with Henrietta?
GEORGE: She's so fucking beautiful, and, when she wants to be, she can be so sweet.
LENNY: Okay. What assumptions are involved?
GEORGE: That this other guy's getting all that sweetness—hey, wait a second. She can also be a Grade A championship bitch, too. And sooner or later he's going to get that side of her, too. (laughter) Then we'll see how long the honeymoon lasts. I'm afraid of that woman, honest to God. When something doesn't go her way, she has a shitfit. In fact, she's pretty much of a spoiled brat.
LENNY: Got that. How's it been handled?
GEORGE: It? How's what been han——oh, yeah, the fact that she's a gorgeous spoiled brat. Well, when she told me to get out, I went quietly. In fact, I packed in a hurry and split, and I felt kind of relieved. She was always getting sick and wanting to be nursed and pampered and taken care of. You know, she can be a very draining woman. But about two days after our first separation, the pain started.

LENNY: I heard that. How's it right now?
GEORGE: It's still pretty awful, but (laughter) I guess I'll survive. . . .
LENNY: Thank you. So—— I'm sorry. . . .
GEORGE: No, I was just going to say, I guess I'll make it, but for a while, I wasn't so sure. I mean, miss her! Oh baby. I used to see her a thousand times a day, but it would just be somebody who looked kind of like her.
LENNY: Got that. So what conditions have you encountered with Henrietta?
GEORGE: Discontent. Restlessness. Huge bills that she was supposed to pay but never would. Irresponsibility—you know, nifty things like that.
LENNY: Okay. What assumptions are involved?
GEORGE: That she adores playing spoiled brat—and also that she's hostile as hell toward men. You know, she's been married about three times, and I don't know how many guys she's shacked up with. She's a female *macho*.
LENNY: Okay. How's it been handled?
GEORGE: I'd get pissed off as hell at her, and we'd fight. She'd never clean up around the house, which she told me she would do; providing I took care of the yard. Also, you know, she was supposed to contribute toward the groceries and cook, you know, if I'd do the dishes. But she wouldn't. It wound up like we were eating out all the time, and guess who paid? Bull*shit*!
LENNY: Got that. How's it right now?
GEORGE: You know, maybe I got off lucky. Um, this other guy has got quite a handful.
LENNY: Thank you. What conditions have you encountered with Henrietta?
GEORGE: Arguments. Wild yelling and screaming matches. Her flirting with other guys at parties—them calling her at our place. *Jealousy*. Yeah.
LENNY: Okay. What assumptions are involved?
GEORGE: That I'm not man enough for her, goddammit!
LENNY: Thank you. How's it been handled?

For the Relationship That Just Won't Go   **161**

GEORGE: It hasn't been. No. I mean . . . I'm all tied up in knots. Let me try again: I hated me for not being . . . whatever she wants. A stud. I thought maybe she wants to be dominated, knocked around. Beat up. Controlled. So I hit her once when we were drunk, and she really lit into me. Called me a coward, and a sadist, and a faggot. And I was so ashamed. I was just trying to give her what I thought she wanted, but, apparently, it wasn't that, either. What was the question?

LENNY: Got that. How's it been handled?

GEORGE: I hated her. I hated me. I hated all women, or I thought I did. Okay: It's been handled bitterly.

LENNY: Thank you. How's it right now?

GEORGE: It's better.

    We are presenting you with this transcription of an actual session to show you what area this drill covers and how a session ought, ideally, to be run. Lenny is a master at these repetitive questioning techniques, and so he stayed with this particular drill only two or three more cycles, at the end of which his client "George" was starting to separate his own anger from his ex-lady's and also starting to wonder if he hadn't lucked out of the entire relationship because "Henrietta" would probably wreak no small amount of havoc with her new boyfriend's life. A great deal of "George's" pain was concerned with his feelings of inadequacy—his notion that the Other Guy was somehow superior to him. The portion of the tape we are not reprinting dealt with George's inadequacies and how he handled them.

    It's worth noting that question *a)* brings the entire problem area into focus; question *b)* brings the aberrant area up for inspection (If you punch me in the nose, then all you've done is punch me in the nose. But if I start assuming that you punched me because I'm really a bad guy and deserved it, then I'm in trouble; to a very large extent, it is what we assume about an event that caves us in); question *c)* is an extremely good one because it infers that no matter how weak and how powerless you feel when faced with a certain event, you are still at one level or another *doing something about it* (if only dramatizing powerlessness); question *d)* keeps bringing the Responder back to present-time, and as such it is invaluable.

What Lenny Fusselman realized about "George" is that he was really heavily caved in about his ex-lady and that, since there was so much emotion going on all over the place, George needed to be run on a heavier drill. The following is, accordingly, just about the heaviest drill that anyone can run about *any* kind of relationship. The uses to which it can be put are infinite. The emotions it summons up are incredible, but the end result of running this drill "long enough" (and, for each person, that duration will be different) is that you get to a place where you can be free of the agony of a terminated relationship. (This one works just as well for someone grieving for another who has died.)

We will pick up the tape again; then afterwards I'll write out both parts of the drill and their commands so that you can see them devoid of rhetoric.

LENNY: Okay. Now, what I want you to do is make a very clear mental image-picture of Henrietta. Can you do that? Can you imagine her standing right here in this room, beside you?

GEORGE: No sweat. I see her everywhere anyway. I mean, it's even gotten so I hate to sleep 'cause I know I'm going to dream about her.

LENNY: Got that. Okay, so mock up or imagine Henrietta standing right here in this room, next to you. Tell me when you have.

GEORGE: Uh huh.

LENNY: Good. Reach for Henrietta. Physically do this.

GEORGE: I don't get it.

LENNY: I get that you don't get it. Reach for her.

GEORGE: . . . .

LENNY: No, no, no, no. Take your arms and physically reach for her. There ya go.

GEORGE: Okay. So what?

LENNY: Good. Hold onto her.

GEORGE: I feel stupid doing this, you know.
LENNY: Got that. Hold onto her. Thank you. Good. Now turn loose of Henrietta.
GEORGE: . . . .
LENNY: Physically turn loose of her. Thank you.
GEORGE: You mean, pretend with my hands to turn her loose?
LENNY: Yep. You just did it, let me acknowledge that. Now withdraw from her.
GEORGE: Okay.
LENNY: Good. Reach for Henrietta.
(George does so.)
LENNY: Thank you. Hold onto Henrietta.
(George does so.)
LENNY: All right. Turn loose of Henrietta.
(George does so.)
LENNY: Thank you. Now withdraw from Henrietta. . . . Thank you. . . .

On the third cycle through this drill, George cracked. He refused to turn loose of Henrietta (who, mind you, was not present in a physical sense). He even started crying, and the crying went on and on. Lenny said nothing, he gave George the space to do his crying in. It took twelve cycles through this part of the drill for George to get to a place where he felt good about Henrietta. In the course of those twelve cycles, George cried copious amounts of tears, became very angry, and then—suddenly—the anger left and he felt provisionally okay about having lost Henrietta. The old insight that he had formerly had about her being a pretty difficult case to handle and "good luck" to his successor came back resoundingly. This time, the assumption could be made that he really meant it. Lenny suggested they take a short break.

After the break Lenny ran through the second part of the drill some seven or eight times:

LENNY: Okay. The session has resumed. Any last words?
GEORGE: I feel a hell of a lot better.
LENNY: Well, in that case, let's go for feeling even better than *that*. Okay?

GEORGE: Let's do it.
LENNY: Okay. Now I want you to mentally create a very solid mental image picture of Henrietta standing right here in this room right now. Let me know when you've got her good and solid.
GEORGE: She's right here beside me, taking off her blouse.
LENNY: Good. Now have Henrietta reach for you. Tell me when you've got her reaching for your bod (*i.e.*, for your body).
GEORGE: Uh huh.
LENNY: Okay. Have Henrietta hold onto you. Tell me when she is.
GEORGE: Ummmm.
LENNY: Good. Have Henrietta turn loose her hold on you. Tell me when she has.
GEORGE: (long pause) Okay.
LENNY: Thank you. Now have Henrietta withdraw from you. Tell me when she has.
GEORGE: (mumbling) I never could tell that broad anything.
LENNY: Got that! Do it anyway. *You* have Henrietta reach for you.
GEORGE: (pause) Okay.
LENNY: Good. Have Henrietta hold onto you. Tell me when you got her holding onto you.
GEORGE: Yes. O Jesus Christ. . . .
LENNY: GOT THAT. Have Henrietta turn loose of you. Tell me when she has.
GEORGE: I'm sorry. I feel like crying some more.
LENNY: It's okay. Cry.

(George does, but not nearly with his former intensity. After a loud nose-blowing, Lenny gives him the following command):

LENNY: All righty. Now have Henrietta withdraw from you. Tell me when she has.
GEORGE: Yeah.
LENNY: Thank you. Have Henrietta reach for you.
GEORGE: Okay.
LENNY: Thank you. Have Henrietta hold onto you . . . that's it, really tight. . . . Good. Okay. Now have Henrietta turn loose of you.

GEORGE: I don't want her to!
LENNY: GOT that. Have her do it anyway.
GEORGE: (long pause) . . . All right.
LENNY: Thank you. Have Henrietta withdraw from you. . . .
GEORGE: It hurts, but it hurts good. It's kind of like jiggling a loose tooth.
LENNY: Thank you. Have Henrietta reach for you. . . .

Why this drill works as powerfully as it does remains a mystery to me. Lenny contends that what the drill does is to have a person duplicate on a conscious, volitional level exactly what he is doing unconsciously anyway. "The apparency," he says, "is that Henrietta is holding onto George, but in actuality George is holding onto her. She appears to be obsessing him. What's really happening is that he is allowing himself to be obsessed by her. Prison bars do not a prison make. And wardens don't make prisons, either; nor do jailers. Each prisoner, rather, makes his own prison. The first part of the drill puts a person to consciously duplicating what he is doing automatically in relation to the person whom he loves and has lost. You'll notice that the emotional fireworks, when they do occur—and they only occur in maybe one out of every two people—usually turn on at the third command: "Turn loose of so and so."* But the tears and the emotional dramatizations are secondary phenomena. What this drill accomplishes is to free a person from automatically grasping somebody else who doesn't want to be grasped or who was unkind enough to up and die. You got that? Okay, now write this down verbatim. This is pure, undistilled wisdom: *Anyone or anything you can't consciously turn loose of has got you.* Anyone or anything you can consciously turn loose of hasn't got you. It's that simple.

---

*"Tell them", my coauthor says, "for God's sake not to be expecting a huge onslaught of emotion, because they'll be disappointed if it doesn't occur. And also tell them that the third command is not necessarily the one that's going to trigger the emotions. There may be no discernible emotional charge blowing off at all in the course of this drill, only after about twenty or thirty minutes of running it, the Responder suddenly brightens up. As a matter of fact, don't even limit it to twenty or thirty minutes.

"What this drill is out to do is to produce change in a grief-locked relationship. If it produces change, then it's working; if it doesn't then it isn't, and they should go on and run something else."

"The second part of the drill," Lenny goes on to say, "is also beneficial because it puts a person to assuming responsibility over the entire relationship. Look at George. Let's face it: He's probably never going to see Henrietta again. She's up and gone. She's moved in with somebody else. That's the fact of the matter. George knows this—and he also *almost* knows that unless he takes control over his part of the relationship with her, 'she's' going to haunt him for a long time to come. Physically, she's gone; emotionally, what's bothering him is that she's still with him. So the second part of this drill puts him to taking control over the mental pictures he has of Henrietta which are tying up so much of his emotional energies. Did you put in that part of the tape where he said that, after she left him, he took to sleeping eighteen hours a day? According to him, that's what he did. He was emotionally exhausted by the struggle to hold onto her *and to keep her holding onto him!* This is the essence of a stuck emotional flow. She's gone. He's left holding the mental image picture bag, and he doesn't want to see how empty that bag is. His future having-ness with her (all the things he'd planned on doing with her) is shot to hell. So he's back compulsively holding onto what they had in the past; this is another factor. In present-time, he's got nothing—he doesn't even have any present-time. Okay? This drill produced change in his stuck relationship with his former lady love. George will be able to go out now and meet another girl or a while bunch of other girls. Hopefully, the games they'll co-create won't be as disastrous.

"Okay, now rap this verbatim, too. This drill will produce change in anyone's relations with someone else provided that it's run long enough. When you're running it on somebody, become very sensitive to his or her rhythm of responding to the commands. You may go ten, twenty, even thirty minutes and the guy you're running on the drill is responding like clockwork; maybe he's even a little bored. Then you give a command, and, all of a sudden, you've lost him. He spaces out completely. Okay, let him do that. After a minute or two you say, 'Are you reaching for Henrietta?' 'Huh? Oh yeah, yeah, yeah,' he tells you. 'Good', you say, 'turn loose of Henrietta.' And he says, 'No!' What you've got here is the certainty that a lot of emotions are going to be surfacing in the near future. So you say, 'I heard that.

I will repeat the command: Turn loose of Henrietta.' And at this point *stick with this drill!* See, what's happened is the guy has been so automatically stuck on Henrietta that she's been right on top of him. He's just kind of pulled a blanket of her over him. And he's used to doing this. Now he's getting to the point where the numbness is wearing off. He's starting to take a look at the actuality of the situation. For God's sake don't leave him sitting in this place, but have him keep running the drill until he is at cause over his relationship with her.

"If the Responder is still hung up on so and so (Henrietta), then he is not at cause over reaching for her, holding onto her, turning loose of her, and withdrawing from her. When he is free to do all this—and he feels good about doing each one of these acts toward her—then he's run the drill long enough.

"And if you *really* want to blast loose of somebody, and you're up to running it, try this version:

a) Reach for that part of you that 'Henrietta' created.
b) Hold onto that part of you that 'Henrietta' created.
c) Turn loose of that part of you that 'Henrietta' created.
d) Withdraw from that part of you that 'Henrietta' created.

"This one is a wild s.o.b. And not everybody's going to be able to do it. Now, nobody creates anything but you yourself; however, the apparency is that *she* created this ulcerous condition in my stomach lining. This offshoot on the drill will handle that."

Just as you cannot force someone to love you, so you cannot make a person who is sitting in a pile of grief examine what his pedestal is made of. So if your partner feels silly doing this drill and refuses to have anything to do with it, and you're sick of acknowledging his gripes, then forget the drill, and move onto the last one in this chapter, which is not nearly as tough to run.

Before getting into it, here are the commands of the drill we've been discussing:

Part One

a) Create a very solid mental picture of _____ .
b) Bring _____ into this room and have him or her stand right next to you. Tell me when you've done this.

c) Okay. Now reach for _____ . Do this physically, *i.e.*, use your arms and hands.
d) Thank you. Hold onto _____ .
e) Thank you. Turn loose of _____ .
f) Thank you. Withdraw from _____ .

    Note that if your partner starts becoming very reluctant to turn loose of his or her Special Other, you can expect an emotional discharge, probably the next cycle around. Allow whoever is being run on this drill to cry or to yell and howl. Do not try to "mother them" here and do not try to play group leader and drive them down further into the pain. Allow them to experience it, pass them a Kleenex, and continue running the drill. The repetition here is what eventually will bring them to a space that is senior to both the relationship itself and its attendant sorrow.

Part Two

a) Create a very solid mental image picture of (the same person who figured in Part One) .
b) Bring _____ into this room and have him or her stand right next to you. Tell me when you've done this.
c) Good. Now have _____ reach for you. Tell me when you've done this.
d) Thank you. Have _____ hold onto you. Tell me when you've done this.
e) Thank you. Have _____ turn loose of you. Let me know when _____ has.
f) Thank you. Have _____ withdraw from you. Tell me when _____ has.

    As we have indicated, this drill, in both its parts, will eventually work for just about anyone. A so-called "momma's boy" or "daddy's girl" who has difficulty going out on his or her own would profit from it immensely, as would their parents. A widow or a widower who is "haunted" (O how the ghost of you clings!) by a former spouse would eventually come to a space where he or she can begin to create a new life full of new relationships simply by being willing to run this drill long enough. And if your "George" is off with a new lady or your "Henrietta" with another man (or your "George" is off with another man and your

"Henrietta" with another lady) and you are miserable because of it, then this drill is made for you. It can work on missing or dead pets. It can work on a job you really liked but lost. All you have to do is be willing to create mental images of your pet or your job (say, your desk over by the water cooler) and then be willing to reach for it, hold onto it, turn loose of it, and withdraw from it . . . then have it do the same for you.

This is the drill that is directly out to put you at cause over the denizens of your mental image universe. I know of few others that yield such high return for the time and effort spent.

If it's too tough to be run, then tackle the next one. And even if you have derived a lot of gain from it, the next drill won't do you any harm to run, either. It is after the same freedom, but its results are usually less dramatic. Ask yourself or have a friend ask you the following questions, repetitively:

a) What about your relationship with _____ are you free to be at cause over?
Response; acknowledgment.
b) What about your relationship with _____ are you *not free* to be at cause over?
Response; acknowledgment.
c) What about your relationship with _____ are you *free not* to be at cause over?
Response; acknowledgment.
d) What about your relationship with _____ are you free to be the effect of?
Response; acknowledgment.
e) What about your relationship with _____ are you *not free* to be the effect of?
Response; acknowledgment.
f) What about your relationship with _____ are you *free not* to be the effect of?
Response; acknowledgment.

This drill is not as dramatic as the one in which the Responder was physically dramatizing his reaching for and holding onto a lost other, but it gets the job done as well. Cause and effect are, as the Lord Buddha taught us, the links in the chain of "karma" that appear to bind us to so many unpleasant aspects of existence, if not bodily existence itself.

If you can arrive at a space where you see and know you are at cause over everything that happens in your universe and are also willing to take responsibility over those areas of creativity where your universe overlaps with the universe of others, you will be freed from a great deal of human bondage. That this particular freedom is not the direct aim of this book should in no way deter from realizing that it exists.

13

Flowing Love

To a larger extent than most of us recognize, our lives are susceptible to the influence of cycles which, while they never totally govern us, are nevertheless able to exert a profound influence on our behavior. One of the most potent of these cycles (think of them as "larger rhythms of nature," if you will) has three parts:

>create,
>destroy,
>and, when destroy doesn't quite work: *create an absence of* (in other words, deny vehemently ever having had anything to do with either the creation or the destruction).

See how this might work with a relationship: In the beginning, boy meets girl, and it's wonderful, and either the boy or the girl is creating the quality which might be described as wonderful. Since everything about the relationship (her beauty, her humor, her warmth—"the way you wear your hat/the way you sip your tea . . .") is wonderful, we might coin a word to describe the feeling involved as that of *wonderful-ness*.

Time passes, and the enchantment wears off. Let's say that the girl meets somebody else toward whom she starts flowing this quality of *wonderful-ness*. What happens to the boy? He's hurt, yes, but what does he usually start creating? *Destroy,* or destruction-ness. There's any number of things he might do, but among them are: ripping her photo up, going around in high dudgeon "just spoiling for a fight", maybe even beating up her or the rival. This doesn't work too well, so finally the boy decides to create an absence of: 'I never loved her. It was all a mistake. She never reached me. I'm going to put the whole thing out of my mind . . . AND I'M NEVER GOING TO GET HURT LIKE THIS AGAIN (though I'm not really hurt—pain? what pain?) AND I'M NEVER GOING TO GET ANYWHERE NEAR LOVE AGAIN!'

These are the computations that do tend to get made on any endeavor about which we become interested enough to risk emotional involvement. Since there are few such endeavors that do not entail emotional involvement, it may be said that this *create-destroy-create an absence of* cycle prevails in just about every sphere of human activity. It is well to be aware of this cyclical mechanism because that immediately gives you some freedom to start overhauling it. Indeed, from a highly abstract point of view, the quality of an individual life depends, in large part, upon where a person is most of the time on any one part of the cycle.

If, for instance, you find yourself chronically *creating an absence of,* then you will also probably find yourself leading a life of material and/or emotional poverty. (That is, *if* you can find yourself creating these absences—to most of us who are in the middle of this part of the cycle, it appears as if "life" and life's conditions were militating against our ever having anyone or anything worthwhile.) But, in truth, we create our own scarcities. (What this has to do with love will become apparent momentarily.) This same "blanket apparency" obtains for those of us who are firmly lodged in a cycle of destruction—try as we might, we will wind up wrecking everything around us. It is almost as if we were obeying the command DESTROY which is flashing through the very fiber of our being at all times. In this state, orgies of destruction take place because, while we are being the effect of this command, we feel that 'I WIN BY DESTROYING.'

That this makes very little rational sense is secondary to the tremendous emotional spree that the command DESTROY (or, to only slightly a lesser extent, the command CREATE AN ABSENCE OF) entails. If we did not have a mind capable of surveying the resulting bleakness we would feel no sense of loss after the fact. But we do, and here is where great areas of the most acute pain reside. 'God! How could I have done that! I'm my own worst enemy. . . .'

How to step off at least two-thirds of this "wheel of suffering" is beyond the range of this present book, but we do know of a very simple and startlingly effective means of bringing virtually anyone into at least hailing distance of the *create* cycle, as far as love is concerned. And, if you will do the following drill for a time, you will probably succeed in removing yourself from automatically creating either *absences of* or *destruction*—oh yes, we create destruction, paradoxically enough.

From a less abstract point of view, we tend to confuse love (especially the receipt of love) with physical survival. Why this should be is fairly obvious: As infants, we are helpless little piles of protoplasm. Love "means" food, warmth, dry diapers, attention, smiles, gentle handling. If we don't get that love, we probably will die and we certainly will suffer. We thus enter life extremely interested in love. And when, as we develop, love comes to include sexual gratification, our interest in it by no means wanes. We program ourselves to receive love, and one of the great shocks that "growing up" entails is that we no longer receive from the world-at-large the love we got as infants simply because we were cute and helpless. It is when we have to go out into this world and compete for love that failures occur and we tend to slide into either the *destroy* mini-cycle ('Love? Who needs it? I'm tough. Let's you 'n me fight') or the *create an absence of* ('I'm married to my job . . .') mini-cycle.

If either the *destroy* or the *create an absence of* mini-cycles worked, or if we could un-program our cell tissue not to respond so blissfully to another's sweet caress, the creation of love would no longer be necessary. But they are too limiting to work for all of the people all of the time, and so there exists in us a real hunger for love.

The drill we are about to show you remedies the absence of love, and it also puts you to creating love consciously. As an antidote to suffering, it is almost unparalleled, and we invite you—indeed, urge you—to take part in it. You have nothing to lose but your chains.

It can be run with two people (or with one person delivering the commands to many people) or you can run it alone. Here it is:

command a) Flow love out.
(Pause for thirty to forty-five seconds while this command is obeyed.)

command b) Thank you. Receive love.
(Pause thirty to forty-five seconds while this command is obeyed, then return to command a.)

Continue working through the two commands in this extremely simple drill until you have created more love than you believed was extant. Since there is no limit to love, you will feel and function immeasurably better when you realize that if there *were* any limits to love, you would be their creator.

Be warned: The possibilities for a so-called "cosmic experience" are inherent in this drill. Notice that we do not ask you to define love or really do anything else other than create an outflow of love and create the receptivity for an inflow of love.

The first time I had this drill run on me (and, thank you, Ms. Bobbie Metcalf, of the Space of Many Mansions Church, in Los Angeles, both for showing me this drill and allowing my co-author and me to use it in this book!) I experienced a *satori*. In other words, I started following my flow of love out into the physical universe and, in effect, went on the kind of voyage the last surviving member of the Jupiter mission in the film *2001* had before waking up in a cosmic hotel room. It was marvelous—there I was, out of my body, flowing at the speed of thought through deep space.

Now, I cannot guarantee that everyone who embarks upon this drill will undergo an exteriorization (or an interiorization—the two are not all that different) of such a dramatically profound nature, but the potential for the infinite is in the two successive commands of this drill—or, to be truthful, the potentiality for the infinite is you, and these commands plus your willingness to obey them, can put you into unimaginably fine spaces which, once you have tasted them, will inevitably alter the entire quality of your life.

My coauthor and I would be most interested to hear what happens to you once you get into this drill for, say, ten minutes a day for x-number of days. If you do experience a *satori* or if your outlook on life begins shifting toward the positive, and you feel like sharing your experiences with us, by all means please write us c/o the publisher.

And if you are prone to nightmares and you hesitate to go to sleep because of all the strangeness you encounter in that state, you might care to make a tape of these two commands and play it at bedtime. Get a machine that automatically shuts off when the tape is finished, and cut a tape fifteen to twenty minutes long in which these two commands,

Flow love out.
(Pause)
Thank you. Receive love.
(Pause)
Thank you. Flow love out, etc.,

are given with half-minute intervals between the commands to allow you to obey them. In any event, do give this little drill a fair chance. It's magic.

14

Goals to Have Together

In the course of this book, we have looked at:
communications problems,
withheld communications,
problems of expectations,
problems of acknowledgment,
problems of blocked flows of creativity,
problems of mis-identification (I don't see you, but, rather,
    a whole host of others whom I either admire a lot or
    hate a lot whom you remind me of),
which leads to problems of dramatization,
and to problems of standards, and
problems of survival,

and we have also touched fleetingly on problems of goals that lead into that two-thirds of a vicious cycle: destroy—create an absence of. The net effect of looking at all the problems that can arise in the course of a relationship is that you are almost staggered by the sheer amount of negativity that can be exchanged between human beings.

But, there really is no limit to love (save those limits we create), and certainly there are those of us who are both able and willing to have an enduring relationship with one other man or one other woman till death do us part. The remainder of the drills in this book are addressed to people who have decided to stick together, for one good reason or another.

Do you recall our saying earlier that most people go out and create problems in order to have solutions? The following drills are designed to put two people to creating problems because these problems are such fun to solve. These are drills designed to create something for the two of you to *have*—before one of you gets bored and goes out looking for a problem to have—like, say, an extramarital affair.

So if you and He or you and She do decide to stick together, sit down and run the following drill on each other. You can either write the questions down on a card or you can pass this book back and forth between you once a drill cycle is complete. Here are the questions that one of you asks the other:

a) How can you contribute to my survival?
b) How can I contribute to your survival?
c) How can you contribute to your own survival?
d) How can I contribute to my own survival?

A somewhat wilder version of this same drill, for people who are able to have reality on the fact that survival is a game, goes as follows.

a) How can you contribute to my game of survival?
b) How can I contribute to your game of survival?
c) How can you contribute to your own game of survival?
d) How can I contribute to my own game of survival?

After you and Your Special Other have run either version of the above drill, you might like to try the following one, which is also a builder of *having*. In this case, the having is goals. Here are the questions and the instructions:

a) In our relationship, what would you like us to be together?
Your partner answers. Write down his or her answer (and also acknowledge it). Then you ask:

b) In our relationship, what would you like us to do together?
Acknowledge the answer and write it down. Then ask:
c) In our relationship, what would you like us to have together?
Acknowledge the answer he or she gives you and write it down, too.
Next you get your Special Other to ask you these same three questions and to write down your answers.
Continue cycling each other through these three questions until you've both made lists and until you've both told each other everything you want to co-create mutually.
Assess these goals for ones which you both desire and which seem attainable. Make a list of these.
Take the first goal on the list, and ask your partner the following questions:
d) What's the first step toward achieving the goal of _____ ?
e) Thank you for telling me that. How are you going to do it?
f) Thank you. When will you start?

Your partner then asks you questions *d)* through *f)* on your goal for the both of you which you both agree on. And, alternating goals, you work your way down this second (mutually agreed upon) list. Please be aware that what you are doing is consciously programming into existence a co-created goal, and that since there are two of you working on it, it stands a very good chance of being realized in the physical universe. Also note that you do not have to follow each of the steps you mention to achieve the goal. Be flexible enough to accommodate circumstance, but continue postulating the goal. Indeed, if you both continue seeing yourselves as *already having it,* you will enjoy working toward it a good deal more.

In another book Lenny and I plan to write, we'll go into the refinements of programming goals into existence in the physical universe. But the steps we have indicated are essentially how "miracles" get produced.

The next drill is a tremendous trust-builder. Each of you takes turns running through its two questions, which are self-explanatory.

Sit down with your Special Other, and ask him:

a) What would you like to know about me that you don't?
He answers; you acknowledge his answer, and then you tell your Special Other what he'd like to know about you but doesn't.
b) Then you ask him: What should I know about you that I don't?
Your Special Other tells you, and you acknowledge his answer.

Stay with this drill until both of your lives are open books to each other. If you are up to running this drill to a valid release point, and so is your Special Other, there is virtually no way your relationship is not going to endure.

Enjoy it.

APPENDIX:

SEXUAL HANGUPS

These drills help with sexual problems. They cover what you have been doing but perhaps shouldn't (as far as results are concerned) and/or what you shouldn't be doing (as far as results are concerned) but have been. Results are the key. If you've got a viable sex life resulting in your enjoyment, don't bother with the drills here. But even if you are winning at sex, doing these drills will probably help you to win more. Your doing them will, in other words, do you no harm.

Communications Drills on Sex
I.   a)   In relation to sex, what have you had trouble expressing?
    b)   Thank you. Express it to me.
    c)   Thank you. Express it to me some more. . . . some more . . . some more . . . some more, etc.

Continue running this drill on your friend until he is willing to tell you any and everything about his sex life. Note that this is not necessarily show and tell time; and telling will suffice.

One thing to look out for—"you" and "I" are good buddies, and I can tell you *anything*... *but* the moment I get out of your presence, I cave in.

So run this drill until your partner can freely communicate his sexual adventures and misadventures to anyone (should he choose to).

II. a) Who have you had trouble expressing yourself to on the subject of sex?

("Well, mommy found these things in my wallet, and I tried to tell her they were just penny balloons, but she got awfully mad. I don't think she's ever forgiven me really....")

    b) Thank you. Mentally create a picture of your mother. Have her stand right here in the room with you, and express yourself to her freely on the subject of sex.

    c) Continue having your partner do this until he is freely communicating with his problem terminal.

    d) Then—if necessary—ask him *who else?*

    e) Have him do the same thing to each and every one of his problem terminals until he is freely flowing communications outward to them all.

III. a) Who has had trouble expressing himself or herself freely to you on the subject of sex?

("Well, gee, every time George gets a bulge in his pants, he crosses his legs, blushes, stutters, and starts asking me who do I think is going to win the pennant this year in the National League.")

    b) Thank you. Mentally create a picture of George. Have him stand here in front of you, and express yourself freely to him on the subject of sex.

    c) Thank you. Who else?

Do the same thing on all the other "who elses."

IV. a) In your experience, who have you observed having difficulties expressing himself or herself freely to another about sex?

("Well, I remember whenever my mother would tell my father that she was having her headaches, he'd just get into an awful mood.")

Appendix: Sexual Hangups

b) Thank you. Mentally create a picture of your mother and father standing right here in this room.
c) If your mother could express herself freely to your father about sex, what would she say?
d) Thank you. Have her express that.
e) Thank you. If your father could freely express himself to your mother about sex, what would he say?
f) Thank you. Have him express that.

V. a) In relation to sex, what has been _____ ?

suppressed   enforced
invalidated   wondered about
inhibited   unfulfilled
protested   superimposed
withdrawn from   someone else's
withdrawn   unable to be fulfilled
withheld   hidden
shelved   rejected
denied   changed
worried about   destroyed
failed   apparently failed

b) Go METHODICALLY through *each* item on the above list.
c) Take the first item on the list—"suppressed." Put it in the blank space provided.
d) Ask your friend the following question:
In relation to sex, what has been suppressed?
e) Get an answer.
f) Than ask: "What could have brought that about?"
g) Get an answer. Then ask: "What assumptions were involved?"
h) Get an answer. Than ask: "How's it been handled?"
i) Get an answer. Then ask: "How is it right now?"
j) Then ask your friend again: "In relation to sex, what has been suppressed?"

Here is a delicate area. If your partner says "nothing," and yet there is something that has been suppressed about sex, you will have missed that item if you buy his story and go onto the next item on the list. If, however, he says "nothing," and there really is nothing else that has been suppressed, but you keep poking around for something that has been, you will invalidate him. You will thus have created an upset.

One way around this impasse is to continue running this item ("suppressed") and asking all the other questions about it—what could have brought that about? What assumptions were involved, etc.—until your partner tells you, "Nothing. In my experience, there is nothing about sex which has been suppressed.")

Then invite him to "invent something about sex that has been suppressed."

If nothing comes really spontaneously—if your partner doesn't suddenly brighten up and say something like, "Gee, you know, I always assumed everybody knew I was keeping that little kink or quirk suppressed!"—then this area has been thoroughly enough examined for you to go on to the next term on the list.

1. In relation to sex, what has been invalidated?
2. Thank you for telling me that. What could have brought that about?
3. Got that. What assumptions were involved?
4. Thank you. How's it been handled?
5. How is it right now?

Continue this same, methodical examination for each of the twenty-one items on the list. Once your partner has looked methodically at each and all of these areas, he ought to be feeling a great deal freer about sex.

VI.   a) Pertaining to sex, who or what else should have been on the above list?
    b) Write down what your partner says. (Your partner might well reply "My mother. She was pretty straight-laced." Or he might say, "My father. He was a terrific rejecter of sex.")
    c) Then ask him:
What about your mother in relation to sex has been _____ ?

Appendix: Sexual Hangups

suppressed invalidated
enforced inhibited
protested wondered about

one item at a time.
- d) Get an answer. Ask him: "What could have brought that about?"
- e) "What assumptions were involved?"
- f) "How's it been handled?"
- g) "How is it right now?"

The Shame of It All

I.
- a) What's not all right about sex?
- b) Thank you. In relation to sex, what failures have occurred?
- c) Thank you. In relation to sex, how have you failed?
- d) Thank you. In relation to sex, how has another failed you?
- e) Thank you. In relation to sex, how has another failed another that somehow affected you?
- f) Thank you. In relation to sex, what have you done that's not all right?
- g) Thank you. In relation to sex, what has another (or others) done to you that's not all right?
- h) Thank you. In relation to sex, what has another done to another (or others to others) that's not all right?

II.
- a) Tell me an upset you've had in relation to sex.
- b) Thank you. What could have brought that about?
- c) Thank you. What assumptions were involved?
- d) Thank you. How's it been handled?
- e) Thank you. How is it right now?

The Biggie

"To facilitate the goal of sex" means to get off, to have an orgasm/multiple orgasms or, if you're not up to those—which many males aren't—just plain to ejaculate.

"To facilitate the goal of sex" can also mean having a family, working yourself to the bone to send the kids through college, defending yourself against in-laws, and *proving your love*.

"To facilitate the goal of sex" means whatever it means to you. This is a very broad area indeed. So have your friend ask you:

a) What have you been, done, or had to facilitate the goal of sex?
b) Ask this question repetitively.
c) Make a list.

(For instance, your friend might say: "Well, I always wanted to marry a really high-class girl, and I know that mothers of high-class girls would like their daughters to marry doctors. So I became an M.D.")

In this example, *becoming an M.D.* is the answer. It's a pretty big item.

Assess the list you and the Responder compile for just such big items as this. Run questions d) through j) repetitively.

Taking one big item at a time, ask your friend to tell you

d) How has (becoming an M.D.) helped you to win in relation to sex?
e) Thank you. How has _____ helped you to avoid losing in relation to sex?
f) Thank you. How has _____ made you right in relation to sex?
g) Thank you. How has _____ made another wrong in relation to sex?
h) Thank you. How has _____ helped to keep you from being wrong in relation to sex?
i) In relation to sex, what has _____ gotten you into?
j) In relation to sex, what has _____ gotten you out of?

Another Biggie

a) What conditions have you created to avoid having sex?
b) Thank you. How does that help you to avoid having sex?
c) Thank you. How's it been handled?
d) Thank you. How's it right now?

A Redundancy

This drill, while it may seem redundant, is for those who have learned by being done. This is a drill for those of you who are experts on sex the same way that General George Armstrong Custer was an authority on Indians.

a) What conditions have you created to facilitate having sex?
b) Thank you. How does that help facilitate your having sex?
c) Thank you. How's it been handled?
d) Thank you. How's it right now?

What Are You Doing Beside Doing What You're Doing?

Read the following list:

marriage	coming
raising a family	orgasms
fostering true love forever	thrills
fucking	illicit orgasms
sucking	love at first sight
s and m	lust at first sight

Find the term or terms which come nearest to what "sex" means to you. If we've missed any, take responsibility for finding it and, once you've found it, put it in the blank space provided.

a) How have you rationalized or justified having _____ ?
b) How did that rationalize or justify your having _____ ?
c) Why did you feel it necessary to rationalize or justify your having _____ ?
d) How has it been handled?
e) How is it right now?

Any one of these drills, or all of them working together, pull off all the bullshit which you and/or another (others) have shoveled onto sex. When you run these drills, you disperse it. All that is left is your freely creating your sexuality.

A Final Closing Note

Before you and a Special Other decide to make a lifetime commitment, ask yourself: "Are his (or her) problems interesting enough to keep me entertained for the rest of my life?" If they are, then you've probably got a winner going in that relationship. If they're not, well, the door is always open. This is a fairly cynical attitude to take, but beings are in this universe for the vast amounts of interesting problems to have and to appear to be had by. Beings do not like to be bored. The Void is serene, and serenity unending can appear rather boring. But that's another story. . . .